Nourished

# Nourished

## The Art of Eating and Living Well

A collection of all natural, gluten-free recipes, insights
and information for a fresh, feel-good life.

Luna Paige Smith

Photography by Spencer Weiner

Printed in the United States of America

Photography Copyright © Spencer Weiner Photography/SAWfoto.com
All rights reserved
Book Design by Jennie Jacobs
Book Editing by Safia Radha Ohlson

ISBN-13:
978-0615624709 (goodwitchbooks)

ISBN-10:
0615624707

Publisher's Cataloging-in-Publication data
Smith, Luna Paige
Nourished : the art of eating and living well by Luna Paige Smith.
p. cm.
Includes index.
1. Cooking-- all natural, gluten-free. 2. Health and Wellness.
3. Sustainable Living

First Edition

# Table of Contents

# Gratitude

Many thanks to all who contributed to the creation of this cookbook, from inception through gestation and into being. I couldn't have done it without the support of everyone's kindness and generosity. Thank you to Spencer Weiner for his brilliant photographs that grace these pages with such visual beauty. To Safia Radha, the high priestess of prose, for her magical way with words and her loving presence. To Jennie Jacobs for her patient and playful design and illustration genius. To all of my clients and patrons who so openly enjoy and support my creative way with food. To my mom for introducing me to the wonders of the kitchen and for all her loving home cooking. To my dad for bringing home the bacon… and ice-cream! To my brother Jason for encouraging me to stay close to my creativity. To my wonderful community of friends and family for all the ways you each uniquely teach and inspire me to live wholeheartedly in service to the deep and delightful nourishment of all beings.

And last but not least, thank you to Mother Nature for her infinite generosity and wisdom.

Peace and love,

Luna

# Dedication

This book is dedicated to the vision of a fulfilled world where no one lacks the sustenance they need to live a healthy, happy life. A world where we protect Mother Nature, revere her wisdom and learn from her how to be generous and regenerative.

This book is dedicated to all who hunger in body, mind and spirit to live a nourished life. It's dedicated to a sense of plenty, be it in the form of a warm smile, a wholesome meal or an encouraging word. It's dedicated to the feeling of abundance that inspires us to bestow love and kindness upon ourselves and each other. It's dedicated to the reminder that amidst the continuous flux of our day-to-day we are capable of creating and sustaining heaven here on earth together.

# Introduction

A well-lived life begins with how we nurture ourselves and our world. The quality of our food, where it comes from and the care and consciousness with which it's grown and prepared are essential to the health and wellbeing of ourselves and the planet. Each page of this book is seasoned with the intention to harvest, savor and sustain the natural goodness of life. It is an ode to Mother Nature's bounty, daring in its simplicity and full of verve for fresh, vital food. Enter at your own risk. Be forewarned that the contents may tickle unruly taste buds and cuddle ravenous cravings into contented submission. Full of vibrant, easy to prepare recipes, *Nourished* will likely ignite the "healthy sensualist" within and demystify the art of eating and living well. So turn the page and join me in saying a big, yummy "Yes!" to a healthy, happy life.

## Going Gluten-Free

Going gluten-free has no doubt become a big trend recently... so what's it all about? Is it just another health food fad or does going gluten-free have real benefits? Experts have made strong connections between gluten and ADHD and chronic fatigue syndrome, showing that when gluten is eliminated, symptoms from those conditions lessen. More and more people are choosing to remove or reduce gluten from their diets as a way to boost energy, lose weight and better cope with chronic health issues such as arthritis. For people diagnosed with Celiac Disease, a completely gluten-free diet is imperative for re-establishing and maintaining good health. For folks like me who have a milder form of gluten sensitivity, there's usually no denying that we simply feel better on a diet with little to no gluten. For years, my relationship to food and diet has been experimental, from strict purist to frenzied foodie and everything in between. My current sense is that it's about creating balance in the way we eat and live. That will mean something different for each of us. My goal is to continue to discover what that looks, feels and tastes like for me. In my choice to cook and eat primarily gluten-free, I aim to create recipes that are so scrumptious and full of nutritional value that there's no sense that anything is missing.

GLUTEN is a protein found in wheat, barley, and rye. It also shows up in many whole grain foods related to wheat such as bulgur, farro, kamut, and spelt. Gluten is found in the average American diet via breads, baked goods and pasta. But it can also hide out in other foods such as processed meats, salad dressings, beer and processed snack foods.

CELIAC DISEASE is a condition caused by a person's reaction to eating gluten. It damages the lining of the small intestine and prevents it from absorbing parts of food that are important for staying healthy.

## About being "Flexitarian"

My style of cooking and eating is what some call "flexitarian." To me that means primarily an organically grown vegetarian diet with a secondary emphasis on meat, eggs and fish. I don't serve animal protein at every meal, and when I do, I go for the highest quality available. I look for animal proteins that are certified organic (meaning free of antibiotics and growth hormones), grass fed, free range and, whenever possible, locally sourced. Throughout the week I stagger my selections amidst a bounty of fresh, organic produce, grains and legumes. I'm not particularly strict about this, but I do believe that being mindful about the quality and quantity of animal products we consume is good for our bodies and the planet alike.

## About Goat/Sheep Dairy versus Cow Dairy

I love good cheese and yogurt, though I gave them up for awhile because they often upset my stomach and produced a lot of mucus in my system. I heard good things about goat and sheep's milk products – that they are naturally homogenized and are more like human mother's milk than cow's milk, which is why they are known to be easier to digest and less likely to cause lactose intolerance. Also – a substantial side benefit – they are usually sourced from small farm operations, which makes them more likely to be humane certified and sustainably produced. I started experimenting with goat and sheep dairy products and found that, indeed, I was able to digest them well with little to no side effects. Now I primarily use goat and sheep products in my cooking, which makes my belly (and taste buds) very happy. I invite you to explore the world of goat and sheep dairy versus cow dairy and see if you notice a difference in how you feel and how the recipes taste.

Five reasons why I prefer goat & sheep dairy over cow dairy:

- Naturally homogenized.
- Easier to digest.
- Less likely to cause lactose intolerance.
- More like human mother's milk than cow's milk.
- Usually sourced from small farm operations.

# Staples To Get You Started

## Your All-Natural, Gluten-Free Pantry

### Herbs, Spices and Seasonings

**Fresh Herbs:** (I always prefer fresh but dried are ok too.)
Windowsill herb garden (page 19):
basil, chives, cilantro, dill, mint, oregano, parsley, rosemary, thyme

### Spices:
bay leaf - *lifts flavor in soups, stews and sauces*
cardamom - *earthy and slightly spicy*
cayenne - *kicks on the heat*
chili powder- *deep smoky chili flavor*
cinnamon (sticks and powder) - *warming, sweet spice*
cloves- *rich, aromatic spice*
curry powder
cumin (whole seeds and powder) - *staple spice for Indian and Mexican food*
garlic (fresh and dried granules)
ginger (fresh and powder) - *warm, spicy and aids digestion*
herbamare - *herb seasoning salt*
mustard seeds (brown) - *tart and spicy*
paprika - *sweet red pepper*
pepper - *fresh ground is always best*
red chili flakes
sea salt - *fine and coarse*
turmeric powder - *warm, peppery and slightly bitter*
vanilla extract

## Good Oils & Fats

coconut butter - *adds creamy richness to smoothies and desserts*
coconut oil - *great butter substitute and high temp cooking oil*
ghee (clarified butter) - *rich nutty flavor, great for high temperature cooking (see page 154)*
nut butters (almond and cashew) - *for spreading and adding richness to sauces, dressings and desserts.*
olive oil - *staple oil for dressings, sauces and light sautéing*
sesame oil (toasted) - *for flavoring and seasoning*
sesame tahini - *great for spreading, adding richness to sauces, dressings and desserts.*
walnut oil (toasted) - *delicious for dressings and drizzling*

## Fermented Favorites

**Vinegar:** *There are a variety of vinegars offering their unique flavors to dressings and sauces. Here are some great ones to explore and have on hand:*

| | |
|---|---|
| apple cider | mirin |
| balsamic | red wine |
| brown rice | ume plum |
| champagne | |

**Tamari soy sauce** (gluten free):
*a good staple seasoning; it adds a salty, sweet flavoring that enhances almost any dish.*

**Miso paste** (fermented soy bean paste):
*a rich base for everything from soup stocks to marinades. There is a wide range of variations available. I usually lean towards the white and red miso.*

## Natural Sweeteners

agave nectar - *light, neutral flavor, great for baking and adding sweetness to sauces, dressings and beverages.*

honey- *Winnie the Pooh loves it... need I say more? Honey is good to have on hand for sweetening sauces, dressing and beverages. Your local farmer's market is a great place to find a variety of delicious wildcrafted honeys.*

maple sugar- *scrumptious for baking and sprinkling.*
maple syrup- *this is my current favorite for baking and desserts.*
molasses - *adds a deep rich flavor, mainly used in baking.*

## Flours, Meals & Powders

almond flour

almond meal

arrowroot powder - thickening agent

baking powder (aluminum-free)

baking soda

buckwheat flour

cocoa powder (gluten free)

oat flour (gluten free)

maca powder

quinoa flour

spirulina powder

tapioca pearls

## Nuts, Seeds & (Dried) Fruits

### Nuts:
almonds

cashews

hazelnuts

macadamia nuts

pecans

pinenuts

pistachios

walnuts

### Dried fruits:
cherries

coconut flakes

dates

goji berries

golden raisins

thompson raisins

prunes

### Seeds:
flax seeds

(whole and ground)

pumpkin

sesame (black & white)

sunflower

## Whole Grains

kasha (buckwheat groats)
millet
oats (gluten-free)
quinoa

## Rice:

aroborio rice
bhutanese red
brown long grain basmati
brown short grain
forbidden black
white jasmine
wild rice

## Beans & Legumes

adzuki
black
garbanzo
Northern white beans
red lentils

## Sea Vegetables

kombu
arame

## Noodles, etc.

polenta
rice noodles
soba noodles

# Windowsill Herb Garden

## Enjoy cooking with fresh culinary herbs year-round.

You can enjoy fresh herbs all year by planting a windowsill garden. Many herb plants will grow quite well in containers and require only minimal care, plus they add a touch of beauty. The best herbs to grow in your windowsill are cilantro, basil, parsley, chives, mint, thyme and lavender. Imagine the pleasure of snipping fresh herbs right in your kitchen!

## Here's how you do it:

1. Make sure you have a sunny windowsill where your herbs will thrive.

2. Purchase some of your favorite small organic herb plants from a local farmer's market or nursery.

3. Get containers that are at least 6-12 inches deep. You can plant multiple herbs in one wide or long container or use at least a six inch pot for individual plants.

4. Use an organic potting mix that is light and well-draining.

5. Put a 2–3 inch layer of potting mix in the bottom of your container(s).

6. Position your herb plants in the container(s).

7. Fill in empty space with the potting mix, pressing it gently around the plants. Be sure to leave about an inch at the top of the container for watering.

8. Water sparingly. Herbs don't like to sit in wet, soggy soil.

9. Snip herbs and use them often. This will help them grow into full and lush plants.

# Nourished by Dawn

"When you arise in the morning, think of what a precious privilege it is to be alive - to breathe, to think, to enjoy, to love."

- Marcus Aurelius

# Breakfast

Quinoa Pancakes

Golden Granola

The Muffins

Fresh Herb & Goat Cheese Frittata

Ginger-Shiitake Congee

Breakfast Crêpes

Banana Buckwheat Breakfast Porridge

# Quinoa Pancakes

serves 4–6

My two little recipe tester friends Leighton (age 6) and Emrys (age 3) helped me perfect this recipe. Kids can be hard to impress when it comes to "healthy alternatives," but I knew I had reached success when Leighton said "I could eat another and another and another." Try adding a cup of finely chopped apple or one large mashed banana to the batter. It will add to both the flavor and moistness of these little hotcakes.

1 2/3 cups quinoa flour
1 3/4 cups Almond Milk (page 44, or if you're short on time, use the store-bought variety)
1 egg, beaten
1 tablespoon agave nectar or maple syrup
1/2 teaspoon cinnamon (optional)
1 tablespoon aluminum-free baking powder
1/2 teaspoon sea salt, heaping
2 tablespoons coconut oil or ghee, melted (plus a little extra for oiling the skillet if needed)

Mix all ingredients together to create pancake batter. Warm another tablespoon of oil in a large skillet over medium heat. If your skillet or griddle is seasoned well and non-stick, you can cook the pancakes without oil. If not, use a teaspoon or two of oil each time you add batter. Ladle batter onto skillet or griddle, making medium sized pancakes. Adjust the heat as needed; usually the first batch needs higher heat than other batches. The bottom of the pancakes should brown in about 2–4 minutes (the batter will begin to show bubbles on top and then you know they are ready to flip). Flip and cook for 2–4 minutes on the other side.

Serve hot with one of the following toppings:

Fresh chopped chives, toasted pumpkin seeds and goat chèvre
Ghee and real maple syrup
Almond butter and sliced banana
Fresh figs, goat yogurt and a drizzle of honey

# Golden Granola

serves 6–8

It's hard not to feel spoiled when I sit down to a bowl of this luxurious granola drenched in fresh Almond Milk (page 44). Topped with fresh fruit, I can barely contain my glee. Bake a big batch for the holidays and give it away as a gift to family and friends. It looks great in a glass mason jar with festive ribbon tied around the rim. Everyone will appreciate the homemade goodness, and it will save you from some of the holiday shopping chaos.

2 1/2 cups gluten-free oats
1/4 cup gluten-free oat flour
1 cup almonds, coarsely chopped
1 cup macadamia nuts, coarsely chopped
1/2 cup sunflower seeds
1 cup dried coconut flakes
1 1/2 teaspoons ginger powder
1 teaspoon sea salt
1/2 cup coconut oil, melted
1/4 cup + 1 tablespoon maple syrup
1 cup golden raisins (optional)

Preheat oven to 350°. Line a baking sheet with parchment paper and set aside. In a large bowl mix all dry ingredients together, except for the golden raisins. Then add the coconut oil and maple syrup and mix well with hands. Transfer mixture to baking sheet and use your hands to spread granola in an even layer. Bake for 10–12 minutes, then rotate pan in the oven and bake for another 10–12 minutes or until granola is crisp and golden brown. Remove baking sheet from oven and allow to cool completely. Then use your hands again to gently break the granola into bite-size clusters. Add golden raisins if desired.

# The Muffins

makes one dozen… sometimes more!

There's something magical about these muffins. I can't quite explain it, you simply have to experience them for yourself. I will say this though: take care in making them. Like any supernatural concoction, they require your utmost witchy attention.

3 cups raw organic almonds, finely ground

1 1/2 teaspoons baking soda

1/4 teaspoon sea salt

1 teaspoon cinnamon

1 teaspoon ginger powder

1 large apple, peeled, cored
  and finely chopped

1 large carrot, trimmed and grated

1 ripe banana

8 dates, pitted

3 eggs

1/2 cup coconut oil, melted

1 tablespoon vanilla extract

1 cup raisins

Preheat oven to 350°.

Use coconut oil to lightly grease a standard size one-dozen muffin tin.

Grind almonds with S-blade in food processor and transfer into large bowl. Add baking soda, sea salt, cinnamon and ginger. Set aside. Add peeled and cored apple to food processor and pulse until finely chopped but not mushy. Transfer to medium bowl. In food processor, switch out the S-blade for the grater plate and grate the carrot. Then add the carrot to the bowl with chopped apple and set aside. In a blender add banana, dates, eggs, coconut oil and vanilla. Blend to a smooth and creamy consistency (with no date chunks). Add wet mixture to dry mixture and stir thoroughly. Then fold in the raisins, apple and carrot. Spoon batter into greased muffin tins and bake for 15–20 minutes or until muffins are lightly browned on top and baked all the way through.

# Fresh Herb & Goat Cheese Frittata

serves 4–6

I love the simplicity of this frittata. It's perfectly satisfying on its own, or if you're in the mood for a heartier breakfast, serve it with a green vegetable and a side of chicken sausage.

2 tablespoons ghee

6 eggs, beaten

1/4 cup goat chèvre, crumbled

1/4 cup goat gouda or cheddar, grated

1 1/2 cups fresh herbs, such as chives, parsley, basil, cilantro, dill (any combo)

sea salt

fresh ground pepper

Preheat oven to 350°.

In a medium-large, oven-proof skillet melt ghee over medium heat. Beat eggs in a medium sized bowl. Add cheese, herbs, sea salt and pepper. Mix together and pour into skillet. Reduce heat to medium-low. Cook for about 10 minutes. Then transfer to oven and bake for 10–20 minutes. Check every 5 minutes to make sure it doesn't get over-baked. It will be done when the top is no longer runny.

Remove from oven and let stand for a few minutes before slicing and serving. This goes great with Lemon-Zest Asparagus (page 82) or Curly Kale & Baby Portabellas (page 78).

# Ginger-Shiitake Congee

serves 4

Congee is a comforting rice porridge popular in many Asian countries. It's typically served for breakfast but can also be used as a healing food to treat colds, flu and digestive ailments, as it requires little energy to digest but is nourishing and tonifying. If your body is feeling off-balance or stressed try a week of this congee for breakfast and see how much better you feel.

**Broth:**

1/2 cup fresh ginger, cut into small chunks

2 green onions, coarsely chopped

4 dried shiitake mushrooms

2 fresh shiitake mushrooms, thinly sliced

1 clove garlic, peeled and sliced

1 1/2 tablespoons mirin

6 cups water

**Congee:**

1 cup short-grain rice, such as Arborio

4+ cups broth

1/2 teaspoon sea salt

4 green onions, finely chopped

tamari, optional for added flavor

toasted sesame oil, optional for garnish

gomasio, optional for garnish (page 155)

Prepare broth by combining ginger, green onions, sliced fresh shiitakes, whole dried shiitakes, garlic, mirin and 6 cups water in a medium-large pot and bring to a boil. Reduce heat to medium-low and simmer 30 minutes. Strain broth and discard all solids except mushrooms. (You should have 4–5 cups broth.) Thinly slice the whole shiitakes and combine with already sliced mushrooms. Set aside.

Prepare congee by placing rice and broth in medium-large pot and bring to a boil. Reduce heat to low and simmer, covered, for 1 1/4 hours or until rice is very soft and porridge-like. Remove from heat, add shiitakes and green onions and let stand 10 minutes. Spoon congee into serving bowls. Dress with tamari, sesame oil and gomasio as you like.

# Breakfast Crêpes

makes 5–6 crêpes

Crêpes are like the French version of a breakfast burrito. They're fun to make and you can fill them with all kinds of delicious surprises. If you're looking for something sweet instead of savory, try filling them with fresh berries and a big dollop of goat yogurt.

**Batter:**

¾ cup organic rice milk - unsweetened

¼ teaspoon sea salt

1 large egg

½ cup buckwheat flour

1 tablespoon ghee, melted

additional ghee for cooking

**Filling:**

1 tablespoon ghee

10 eggs, beaten

1 cup creamy chèvre goat cheese

2 ripe avocados, pitted and
   thinly sliced

1 vine ripened tomato - chopped

Put rice milk, salt, and egg in a blender and mix on medium speed for 15 to 20 seconds until combined. Add buckwheat flour and melted ghee. Mix on high for a minute. Refrigerate for one hour before using. Heat a medium-large nonstick pan over medium heat. The pan should be hot enough to make the batter lightly sizzle but not too hot or the batter won't spread easily. Use your first crêpe as a way to gauge the heat. Increase or decrease temperature as needed. Add 1/3 cup batter to the pan and swirl to evenly distribute the batter across the bottom of the pan. Cook until the bottom is browned and can be easily flipped, about 3–5 minutes. Then turn crêpe and cook on the other side. Stack cooked crêpes with wax paper between them. This will keep them from sticking together. Wrap them in foil to keep warm in the oven.

Heat ghee in large skillet over medium heat. Add beaten eggs and a sprinkle of sea salt and fresh ground pepper. Cook, folding frequently until they are fluffy and not runny. Remove crêpes from oven, smear them with chèvre and fill with scrambled eggs. Top with tomatoes and avocado slices and fold the edges over each other lengthwise.

# Banana Buckwheat Breakfast Porridge

serves 4

Kasha is the whole groat form of buckwheat. It has a lovely, sweet and earthy flavor and cooks up into a perfect porridge-like consistency making it a nice alternative to oatmeal.

1 cup kasha (toasted buckwheat groats)

2 cups water

1 cup Almond Milk (page 44) + 1 cup for topping

1 cinnamon stick

1 teaspoon vanilla extract

2 bananas, peeled and thinly sliced

1 tablespoon ghee per bowl

maple syrup or honey for drizzling

1/2 cup toasted nuts, such as pecans, walnuts or hazelnuts

Place kasha in a fine mesh strainer and rinse. Add to a medium pot along with 2 cups water, 1 cup almond milk, cinnamon stick, vanilla and a pinch of sea salt.

Bring to a boil then reduce heat, cover and simmer for 10–12 minutes. Remove from heat, leave the lid on and let sit for 5 minutes. Discard cinnamon stick and spoon servings into bowls. Add toppings and enjoy!

# Nourished by Nectar

"A smile is the beginning of peace."

- Mother Theresa

# Drinkables

Cloud Nine Nectar

Heartbreak Shake

Mango Sunrise

Super Green Smoothie

Almond Milk

Wildflower Honey & Meyer Lemonade

# Cloud Nine Nectar

serves 1–2 (if you're willing to share)

This really is the closest thing to heaven I've ever tasted. And don't worry about getting too attached to an esoteric ingredient - most health food and Asian grocery stores stock Thai coconuts.

1 Thai coconut

To open the coconut turn coconut on it's side with top facing out. With a large chef's knife shave the husk of the coconut off to expose the hard shell. Then turn coconut up right. Place your non-dominant hand around the base of coconut to safely hold it in place. Using the lower tip of a butcher knife aim for the tip of the coconut shell and swiftly puncture and then pry open the top. Once you have safely opened the coconut, pour coconut nectar through a mesh strainer into a blender. Scoop out the coconut "meat" with a spoon, making sure no hard shell bits are attached. Add coconut "meat" to blender and blend until creamy smooth. Pour into a tall glass and enjoy.

# Heartbreak Shake

makes 2 pint-glass servings

The name pretty much says it all. This decadently wholesome shake is a real charmer, capable of producing the best kind of heartbreak - one that cracks you open to the excruciatingly delicious pleasure of being alive. It will leave you feeling well-loved and well-fed from the very first sip and keep you coming back for more.

1 pack of acai frozen concentrate (Sambazon pure unsweetened)

1/2 cup frozen strawberries

1 cup frozen blueberries

1 banana

1/2 avocado

4 prunes, pitted

1 date, pitted

1 tablespoon almond butter

1 1/2 cups Almond Milk (page 44) or fresh Cloud Nine Nectar (page 37)

Add ingredients to blender and blend until creamy smooth. Pour into tall pint glasses and enjoy.

You also can play around with adding some super foods to boost the potency of your shake if you like. Who knows? They may even imbue you with super powers.

Try any or all of these:
- 1 tablespoon maca powder for a mood and energy lift
- 1 teaspoon spirulina powder for boosting your immune system
- 2 tablespoons raw cacao nibs for passion and positive self esteem
- 1 tablespoon bee pollen for stamina, endurance and overall well-being

# Mango Sunrise

serves 2–4

This smoothie makes me smile. It's just so pure and delicious – a great reminder of how sublime simple pleasures can be. It tastes like a creamsicle with a blissful tropical twist.

1 young Thai coconut, blended (Cloud Nine Nectar, page 37)

1 ripe mango, cubed

half of an orange, juiced

1 tablespoon fresh lemon juice

1 teaspoon fresh ginger, peeled and minced

Place all ingredients in blender and blend until smooth. Pour into glasses and enjoy!

Feeling anxious? Fresh mango can help. It is a rich source of vitamin-B6 which is required for GABA hormone production in the brain. The GABA hormone plays an important role in balancing the nervous system and creating a calming and quieting effect on the body and mind.

# Super Green Smoothie

serves 4

This is what I imagine green velvet would taste like if it were a nourishing drink. Fresh and luscious, this luxe smoothie is a great way to fuel up on vitamin and mineral rich greens while feeling healthfully indulgent. The avocado and banana give it a creamy, rich texture, while the mango and dates add subtle sweetness, and the mint and cilantro provide a refreshing finish.

1/2 ripe avocado

1 small banana

1/2 ripe mango, cubed

4 Medjool dates, pitted

6 large mint leaves

1/2 cup chopped cilantro

5 large kale leaves, stem removed

Add all ingredients to blender. Then fill the pitcher 2/3 full with water. Blend until creamy smooth. Add more water if it's too thick and blend well. Pour into a tall pint glass and enjoy.

# Almond Milk

makes 3 cups

Fresh almond milk is such a delightful treat to have on hand. It makes a wholesome base for any smoothie and is a great non-dairy creamer for hot tea or coffee.

1 cup raw organic almonds

3 cups water

1–2 teaspoons maple syrup (optional)

Place almonds in a bowl and cover with water to soak overnight. In the morning, strain and rinse them. Place in a blender with water and maple syrup. Blend on high until smooth. Over a large bowl, slowly pour mixture into a nut milk bag or a large sieve. If using a nut milk bag, keep a tight closure on top of the bag and squeeze as much milk out as you can. If using a sieve, coax the liquid through using a spoon or rubber spatula, careful not to let any pulp escape. Once you've extracted as much milk as possible, transfer liquid into a pitcher or glass jar. You can enjoy immediately or refrigerate for later. Almond Milk will keep for about three days.

# Wildflower Honey & Meyer Lemonade

serves 6–8

On a warm day this is a great thirst quencher. On a hot day it transforms into delicious popsicles if frozen. And when the weather is chilly, add two tablespoons of minced ginger, bring to a boil and simmer for 10 minutes for a soothing digestive tea.

1 cup fresh Meyer lemon juice

¾ to 1 cup local wildflower honey

2 quarts of water

Mix the honey and lemon juice in a small saucepan. Warm slightly until the juice and honey meld together easily. Pour juice and honey mixture into a large pitcher and fill with about two quarts of water. Stir until well combined. Refrigerate until cold and serve on ice.

# Nourished by Simplicity

"Simplicity is the ultimate sophistication."
- Leonardo da Vinci

# Soups

Basic Chicken Stock

White Bean & Rosemary Soup with Fresh Spinach

Farmer's Carrot Soup with
Kale Ribbons & Toasted Pepitas

Vietnamese PhoGà

Gentle Green Soup

Adzuki Bean & Ginger Root Stew

Cauliflower & Kabocha Squash Chowder with Fresh Dill

Red Lentil Dahl

# Basic Chicken Stock

serves 6

After you've enjoyed the Lemon-Rosemary Roast Chicken (page 121), save the carcass to make stock. If you don't want to use the carcass right away you can wrap it up and keep it in the freezer for up to four weeks. Making homemade chicken stock is so simple, and it's always far better in taste and quality than store-bought broths.

celery

carrots

onion

parsley

sea salt

fresh ground pepper

water

leftover chicken carcass

Put the leftover carcass - bones, skin and meat from a whole roasted chicken - into a large stock-pot. Add chopped veggies such as celery, onion and carrots (about 2–3 cups each) and several sprigs of parsley. Add about a teaspoon of sea salt and 1/4 tsp of pepper. Add enough cold water to cover 1–2 inches above the ingredients. Bring to a boil and immediately reduce heat to bring the stock to a light simmer. Simmer uncovered for at least 4 hours to get a nice, rich flavor. The longer you simmer, the more concentrated the stock will be. Discard the veggies and carcass and strain the stock through a fine mesh strainer.

Stock can be covered and stored in the refrigerator for 2–3 days or frozen for several months. Be sure to cool before storing.

# White Bean & Rosemary Soup with Fresh Spinach

serves 4–6

Rosemary and white beans might very well be soulmates - when they come together, it's apparent they were made for each other.

2 cup white beans (cannellini), soaked 6–8 hours

1 1/2 tablespoons ghee

1 large yellow onion, diced

6 cloves of garlic, peeled and minced

4 cups chicken broth (page 48)

3 cups water

2 sprigs rosemary + 1 tablespoon finely minced

1 1/4 teaspoons sea salt

fresh ground pepper

1 tablespoon fresh lemon juice

3 cups fresh spinach leaves

Prepare onion, garlic and rosemary. In a large pot melt ghee over medium heat. Add onion to the pot and sauté for 5 minutes. Add garlic and sauté about 5 more minutes, until onions are lightly browned. Strain and rinse the beans and add them to the pot along with the broth, rosemary sprigs and sea salt. Bring to a boil on high heat, then reduce heat to low and simmer for 30–40 minutes until beans are tender. Remove rosemary sprigs. Transfer about 2 cups of soup to a blender and blend until smooth. Return mixture to soup pot. Stir in lemon juice, minced rosemary and spinach and simmer for 3–5 minutes until spinach is lightly wilted. Add sea salt and pepper to taste. Serve hot with freshly baked Almond Bread (page 148).

# Farmer's Carrot Soup with Kale Ribbons & Toasted Pepitas

serves 4–6

If there's a local farmer's market or farm stand where you live I suggest buying your carrots there. They will typically be fresher and tastier than the organic carrots you'll find at the grocery store and will enhance the overall flavor of this vibrant soup.

3 tablespoons ghee

6 cups farmer's carrots, coarsely chopped

1 small yellow onion, peeled and chopped (approximately 1 cup)

1 tablespoons fresh ginger root, peeled and diced

4–5 cups water

1 teaspoon sea salt

1 teaspoon red miso paste

5 large kale leaves, cut into thin ribbons

1 cup pumpkin seeds or pepitas, toasted

In a medium-sized soup pot melt 2 tablespoons of ghee over medium-high heat. Add onions and ginger and sauté 3–5 minutes or until onions are translucent. Add carrots, sea salt and enough water to barely cover the vegetables. Bring to a boil, then reduce heat and simmer for 15 minutes or until carrots are tender. Allow mixture to cool slightly before transferring in batches to a blender. Once the carrot soup mixture is blended, pour it back into the pot and set aside. In a large sauté pan toast pumpkin seeds over medium heat until golden brown. Transfer seeds into small bowl and set aside. Using the same pan, melt remaining 1 tablespoon ghee over medium-high heat. Add the kale ribbons and sauté for about 5–7 minutes, stirring frequently. Kale should be tender yet still bright. Taste the soup and add additional sea salt as needed. Ladle warm soup into bowls, top with kale ribbons and pumpkin seeds and serve.

# Vietnamese Pho Gà

serves 6

Light and tangy broth with a hint of toasted sesame, this dish is filled with fresh herbs, veggies and delicate slices of chicken nestled in a swirl of tender rice noodles. All of which make for a delightfully exotic twist to old-fashioned chicken noodle soup.

1/4 pound rice noodles, cooked

1/4 cup fresh ginger, peeled and minced

2 jalapeño peppers, de-seeded and minced

2 medium carrots, peeled and cut
   into matchsticks

2 cups snow peas, ends cut

4 scallions, white and light green parts
   thinly sliced

1/2 cup fresh cilantro, lightly chopped

1/2 cup fresh mint, thinly sliced into ribbons

1 1/2 cups bean sprouts, rinsed

8 cups chicken broth (page 48)

3/4 teaspoon sea salt

1 pound boneless, skinless chicken breast,
   sliced in thin strips

1 1/2 tablespoons coconut oil

2 tablespoons toasted sesame oil

1 1/2 tablespoons tamari soy sauce

1–2 tablespoons fresh lime juice, + 1 lime cut
   in 6–8 wedges

Cook rice noodles by following instructions on package. Once they are cooked transfer them to a colander, rinse under cold water and set aside. (I suggest cooking them slightly *al dente* so they will hold up nicely in the hot soup.) Prepare ginger, jalapeños, carrots, snow peas, bean sprouts, cilantro, mint and chicken and set aside. In a large pot melt 1/2 tablespoon of coconut oil over medium-high heat. Add ginger and sauté for 1–2 minutes. Add chicken broth and sea salt and bring to a boil. Reduce heat to low and simmer for 5 minutes. Add carrots and jalapeños and simmer for 7–10 minutes more. Meanwhile, in a large skillet melt remaining coconut oil over medium-high heat. Add chicken and sauté until just cooked through. Using tongs, transfer cooked chicken to soup pot along with snow peas and bean sprouts. Add tamari, sesame oil and lime juice and simmer for 5–7 minutes, just until the snow peas turn tender and bright green. Taste soup and add more sea salt and lime juice as needed. Then place equal portions of rice noodles in six bowls. Ladle soup over the noodles and garnish with scallions and fresh herbs. Serve with lime wedges.

# Gentle Green Soup

serves 4

I hesitated at first to include this recipe, thinking it didn't pack the same "star quality" as my other soup favorites. Then my digestion got a little out of whack and I was a bit run down, so I made a batch of the Gentle Green Soup and was immediately reminded of how wonderfully healing it is. Packed full of vitamin and nutrient rich broccoli, spinach and zucchini, it's an easy, tasty way to get your daily dose of green vegetables.

1 large zucchini, cut into large chunks (3 cups)

1 medium head of broccoli, cut into small florets (4 cups)

7 cups (packed) fresh spinach, washed

4 cups water

sea salt to taste

In a medium-large pot add zucchini, broccoli and water. Bring to a boil, then reduce heat and simmer for about 7 minutes until vegetables are tender and bright green. Remove from heat and set aside to cool for about 15 minutes. Then transfer to blender and blend on high until smooth. Add fresh spinach in batches and purée until all ingredients are thoroughly blended. Return mixture to pot, add sea salt to taste and simmer on low for 5 minutes to warm. Then serve in mugs or bowls and enjoy. I like to sip it from a mug with a sprinkle of gomasio (page 155) on top.

# Adzuki Bean & Ginger Root Stew

serves 6

Subtly sweet and nutty in flavor, the nutrient-rich Asian adzuki bean is revered for its blood nourishing properties. This rich, earthy stew shows the bean off beautifully. On a chilly day I love cozying up to a bowl of it with a thick slice of almond bread (page 148).

2 cups adzuki beans (soaked overnight)

3 cups cubed kabocha squash (seeded, unpeeled)

6 cups water

4 cups kale (thin strips)

1 three inch piece of kombu

1–2 tablespoons ginger root (peeled, finely chopped)

1 teaspoon sea salt

1 1/2 tablespoons tamari

sprinkle of gomasio (page 155)

Soak adzuki beans overnight, strain and rinse. In a medium pot, add beans, water, salt and kombu. Cover and bring to boil, then reduce heat to low and simmer for 45 minutes. Add kabocha squash and ginger. Simmer for 10 minutes. Add kale. Simmer for 5 minutes. Add tamari. If you prefer a thinner stew add warm water, salt and tamari to taste. Garnish with gomasio.

Chef's Note: Adding kombu seaweed while cooking beans will help tenderize and make them more easily digestible.

# Cauliflower & Kabocha Squash Chowder with Fresh Dill

serves 6

I invented this soup while doing a cleansing diet consisting of mostly vegetables. After many days of nothing but veggie juices and puréed soups, I just wanted something I could sink my teeth into. I opened the refrigerator and grabbed what was there and voilà! This wonderful chowder came to be.

3 cups kabocha squash, seeded and cut into 1 inch cubes

1 medium head of cauliflower, coarsely chopped

2–3 teaspoons sea salt

1 tablespoon fresh ginger, peeled and finely diced

1 1/2 tablespoons fresh lemon juice

1 cup fresh dill, chopped

2–3 cups of baby spinach

Wash and prepare vegetables. In a large pot place chopped cauliflower and enough water to just cover it. Add 2 teaspoons of sea salt and bring to a boil over high heat. Then reduce heat to low, add ginger and kabocha and simmer for 15–20 minutes. Veggies should be tender but not mushy. Transfer roughly half the soup to a blender and blend until smooth. Return mixture to pot. Add lemon juice, dill and spinach and stir gently to combine. Simmer for about 5 more minutes until spinach is wilted. Taste and add sea salt as needed. You can also add extra lemon juice if you'd like a bit more tang. Serve hot with fresh Almond Bread (page 148) and Carrot Butter (page 152).

# Red Lentil Dahl

serves 6

This is one of my favorite one-pot meal staples. I sometimes make a batch for the week and eat it for breakfast, lunch and dinner, as is the habit in India. Red Lentil Dahl is filling, nourishing, inexpensive and full of warming spices that make the belly very happy.

1 tablespoon ghee

1 tablespoon cumin seeds

1 small yellow onion, chopped (about 1 cup)

1 1/2 cups red lentils, rinsed

5 cups water

1 teaspoon sea salt

1 teaspoon turmeric powder

3 small carrots, diced (about 1 /1/2 cups)

1 1/2 tablespoon fresh ginger, peeled and finely diced

4–6 chard or kale leaves, thinly sliced (2 cups-packed)

1 tablespoon fresh lemon juice

1 cup cilantro, chopped

In a medium soup pot melt ghee over medium-high heat. Add cumin seeds and sauté for 1 minute. Stir in onion and sauté for 5–7 more minutes until lightly browned. Add lentils, water, sea salt and turmeric. Raise heat to high, cover pot and bring to a boil. Then reduce heat to low and simmer partially covered for 10 minutes. Add carrots and ginger and simmer for 10–15 minutes more, until the lentils and carrots are tender. Add chard or kale and simmer for 5 minutes until it's tender too. Stir in lemon juice. Taste and add sea salt as desired.

Garnish with cilantro and enjoy.

# Nourished by Beauty

"Everybody needs beauty as well as bread,
places to play in and pray in, where nature may
heal and give strength to body and soul."
                                        - John Muir

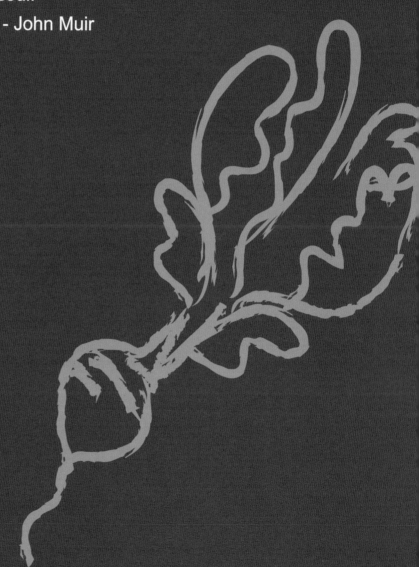

# Salads

Thai Shredded Veggie Salad with Citrus Tahini Dressing

Summer Bean & Radicchio Salad with Walnut Vinaigrette & Shaved Manchego

Avocado Caesar Salad with Garlic Toasted Walnuts

Baby Cucumber, Sweet Corn & Arame Salad

Zucchini Ribbons with Pine Nuts & Pecorino Romano

Asparagus, Hearts of Palm & Heirloom Cherry Tomato Salad

Wild Arugula with Orange, Pecans & Shaved Fennel

# Thai Shredded Veggie Salad with Citrus Tahini Dressing

serves 6

Loaded with vital, fresh veggies, this is a deliciously light yet hearty salad. If you'd like a bit more to sink your teeth into add some grilled, sliced chicken on top.

4 large romaine leaves, cut into thin ribbons

1 1/2 cups purple cabbage, shredded

2 cups bean sprouts

1/2 red bell pepper, de-seeded and cut
    into thin strips

1 cup snow peas, trimmed and thinly sliced

1 cup cilantro, chopped

1/2 cup mint, cut into thin ribbons

3 scallions, thinly sliced

Place all prepped salad ingredients in a large bowl and thoroughly combine. Plate individual servings and drizzle with tahini dressing (see below).

**Tahini Dressing:***

1/2 cup tahini

1/2 cup water

1 tablespoon lemon juice

1 tablespoon apple cider vinegar

1 tablespoon tamari soy sauce

1 small clove of garlic

1/2 teaspoon sea salt

Blend all dressing ingredients in a blender until creamy smooth. Adjust flavor as needed.

*Yields about 1 1/4 cups of dressing. Dressing will thicken as it sits in the refrigerator, so just add a little water to thin it out. I love this dressing on salads, drizzled on top of steamed vegetables and grains, and it's great as a dip for veggies when it's thick.

# Summer Bean & Radicchio Salad with Walnut Vinaigrette & Shaved Manchego

serves 6

When I first discovered toasted walnut oil I put it on everything. I couldn't get enough of it. The taste is sensational in salad dressings, sauces and smoothies.

1 tablespoon peeled and minced shallot

4 1/2 teaspoons red wine vinegar

1 teaspoon dijon mustard

1/4 cup olive oil

1 tablespoon toasted walnut oil

3 cups green string beans, trimmed

3 cups yellow string beans, trimmed

1 cup radicchio, chopped in thin ribbons

1 cup walnuts, toasted and chopped

2 ounces manchego cheese

Whisk together first five ingredients in small bowl and set aside. Place green beans in a large skillet and cover with water. Bring to a boil over medium-high heat. Then reduce heat to low and simmer until they're tender-crisp.

Strain beans in a colander and run under cold water until cool, then place them in a large bowl. Add radicchio, toasted walnuts and vinaigrette and toss together. Season with sea salt and freshly ground pepper to taste. Using a vegetable peeler shave thin slices of manchego over the salad and serve.

# Avocado Caesar Salad with Garlic Toasted Walnuts

serves 4–6

Although I love a traditional caesar salad, I have to admit I'm not a fan of anchovies. In fact, they make me cringe a little. I much prefer avocados. To me they are pure decadence… and it's impressive how they whip up into such a rich, creamy texture. They make the perfect base for this mock-caesar dressing.

1 head romaine lettuce, torn or chopped into bite-size pieces (12 cups)

**Dressing (makes 1 cup):**

1 ripe avocado

3 tablespoons fresh lime juice

2 tablespoons olive oil

1/2 teaspoon dijon mustard

1 clove of garlic

1/2 teaspoon cumin powder

1/2 teaspoon sea salt

pinch of cayenne (optional)

1/4 to 1/2 cup water

**Garlic Toasted Walnuts:**

1 1/2 cups walnuts

1 1/2 teaspoons garlic granules

1 teaspoon sea salt

2 tablespoons olive oil

Preheat oven to 350°. Prepare dressing by blending all ingredients in a blender until creamy smooth. Add remaining water if necessary. Prepare Garlic Toasted Walnuts by lining a baking sheet with parchment paper. Combine all toasted walnut ingredients in a bowl and mix well with hands. Transfer to the baking sheet and spread out in a single layer. Bake in the oven for approximately 10 minutes or until walnuts are lightly toasted. Remove from oven and transfer to a plate to cool.

Place romaine in a salad bowl and toss with dressing. Serve topped with toasted walnuts. Diced tomatoes are also a nice accent for this salad.

# Baby Cucumber, Sweet Corn & Arame Salad

serves 4–6

I like to use baby cucumbers in this dish because their skin is delicate and sweet so there's no need for peeling, plus the bright green adds color. If you can't find baby Persian cucumbers, substitute a regular large cucumber. Just be sure to peel and de-seed before dicing. Sometimes I like to toss in a handful of finely chopped fresh mint.

2 ears fresh corn, shucked and cut off the cob

4 baby Persian cucumbers, quartered lengthwise and cut into small chunks

1 cup arame, soaked for 10 minutes, drained and rinsed, then coarsely chopped

1/4 cup fresh basil leaves, cut into thin strips

1/4 cup red onion, finely diced

2 tablespoons rice vinegar

1 tablespoon toasted sesame oil (optional)

3/4 teaspoon sea salt

Combine all ingredients in a large bowl and mix thoroughly. Serve room temperature or chilled.

# Zucchini Ribbons with Pine Nuts & Pecorino Romano

serves 4–6

When zucchini is in season it grows abundantly, and this is a great way to make use of its vibrant generosity. This dish has delicate elegance and earthy charm. So simple to prepare, yet somehow it comes across as sophisticated.

1/3 cup olive oil

2 tablespoons fresh lemon juice

1 teaspoon coarse sea salt

1/2 teaspoon freshly ground pepper

2 pounds medium zucchini - trim the ends

1/4 cups toasted pine nuts

1/4 cup chopped parsley

small wedge of Pecorino Romano cheese

Whisk oil, lemon juice, sea salt and pepper in small bowl and set aside. Using a vegetable peeler and working from top to bottom of each zucchini, slice zucchini into thin ribbons. Place ribbons in a large bowl. Add the parsley, pine nuts and dressing. Toss together and season with sea salt and pepper to taste. Using the fine side of grater, grate Pecorino Romano over the salad and serve.

# Asparagus, Hearts of Palm & Heirloom Cherry Tomato Salad

serves 4 – 6

Craving a fresh and simple summertime salad? Here it is. What a tasty compliment to grilled meat or fish, and it's equally satisfying all by itself. For an extra kick I sometimes like to top it off with half a cup of crumbled goat or sheep's feta.

1 pound asparagus, trimmed

6 cups heirloom cherry tomatoes, halved

1 (15 ounce) can of hearts of palm, cut in 1/2 inch rounds

1 cup fresh basil leaves, thinly sliced

1–2 cloves of garlic, minced

1/4 cup olive oil

2 teaspoons fresh lemon juice

2 teaspoons dijon mustard

1/2 teaspoon sea salt

1/4 teaspoon fresh ground pepper

Place asparagus in a large skillet with just enough water to cover. Bring to a boil and blanch for two minutes. Drain and rinse immediately with cold water until asparagus is cool. Cut at an angle into 1 inch pieces. Place in a large bowl with tomatoes, hearts of palm and basil and set aside. In a small bowl whisk together all remaining ingredients. Pour into large bowl with vegetables and mix well to coat everything evenly with dressing. Serve at room temperature or chill for a few hours and then serve.

# Wild Arugula with Orange, Pecans & Shaved Fennel

serves 6

This salad is as much a feast for the eyes as it is for the tastebuds. During the holiday season my friends and I always gather for a festive, family-style potluck, and this dish has been a shining star on our bountiful table.

6 cups arugula, rinsed

2 large oranges, peeled and white pith cut away, sliced into rounds, then quartered

1 large fennel bulb, quartered lengthwise, cored and sliced paper thin crosswise

1 1/2 cups toasted pecans

1 cup pomegranate seeds (when in season, for garnish)

1 cup crumbled sheep feta (optional, for garnish)

**Dressing:**

juice of half an orange

1 1/2 tablespoons champagne vinegar, white balsamic or white wine vinegar

3 tablespoons olive oil

1 small shallot, peeled and minced (approximately 1 tablespoon)

sea salt and fresh ground pepper to taste.

In a large bowl add arugula, oranges, fennel and pecans. Prepare dressing by whisking together dressing ingredients in a small bowl. Pour dressing over salad and toss to thoroughly combine. Place portions of dressed salad on individual plates are garnish with pomegranate seeds and feta.

# Nourished by Nature

"I thank you God for this most amazing day, for the
leaping greenly spirits of trees, and for the blue
dream of sky and for everything which is natural,
which is infinite, which is yes."

- E.E. Cummings

# Veggies

Summer Squash Au Gratin

Curly Kale with Baby Portabellas

Simple Mashed Potatoes

Curried Cauliflower & Leeks

Asparagus Spears with Lemon Zest

Roasted Brussel Sprouts with Marcona Almonds

Green Beans & Carrots with Mustard Seeds

# Summer Squash Au Gratin

serves 6

Sautéed summer squash with garlic and onion is just plain good. But I couldn't resist embellishing with creamy, rich goat chèvre layered between the sweet and tender slices of squash to achieve a beautiful display of sinful purity.

2 tablespoons coconut oil

1 medium large yellow onion, peeled, cut in half and sliced thin

2 cloves garlic, peeled and minced

8–10 medium yellow crookneck squash (3 pounds), trimmed and sliced in thin rounds

1/3 cup fresh chives, finely chopped

6 ounces crumbled chèvre goat cheese

sea salt and fresh ground pepper

Preheat oven to 375°. In a large skillet, melt coconut oil over medium-high heat. Add onions and sauté 3 minutes. Add garlic and sauté 5–7 minutes, until onions are lightly browned. Add squash, sprinkle generously with sea salt and pepper and sauté for 7–10 minutes, until they release their juices and become tender. Remove from heat. In a two-quart glass baking dish place a layer of the squash mixture. Then sprinkle with chive and goat cheese. Repeat layering until all ingredients are used up. Place in oven and bake for 20–25 minutes. Remove from oven and let stand for 5–10 minutes before serving.

# Curly Kale with Baby Portabellas

serves 4

Kale is the ruling member of vegetable royalty. It's a powerhouse like no other, full of essential nutrients the body needs to thrive. If you're not already a fan become one! Your body will thank you.

2 tablespoons coconut oil

6 baby portabella mushrooms, washed and sliced thin

2 tablespoons tamari

1 bunch curly kale, stem removed and torn into bite size pieces

In a large skillet, melt coconut oil over medium high heat. Add mushrooms and sauté for 5 minutes, until lightly browned and tender. Add 1 tablespoon tamari and sauté 2–3 minutes more. Then add kale to skillet, reduce heat to medium and cover. Steam for 5 minutes. Remove lid, add remaining tablespoon of tamari and stir well to thoroughly combine. Sauté for 5 minutes more, until kale is tender. Serve warm with Lemon-Rosemary Roast Chicken (page 121) and Simple Mashed Potatoes (page 79).

# Simple Mashed Potatoes

serves 6

This is comfort food at its finest – and healthiest. These potatoes are easy to whip up and make a very versatile side dish.

5 large russet potatoes

3/4 cup canned coconut milk

2 tablespoons ghee

sea salt

fresh ground pepper

Peel, rinse and chop potatoes into medium-sized cubes. Place in medium-large pot and add 1 teaspoon of sea salt and just enough water to cover potatoes. Bring to a boil then reduce heat and simmer until potatoes are tender, about 25 minutes. When potatoes are done, drain well and return them to the pot. Add the canned coconut milk and ghee and mash them with a fork or potato masher. Add sea salt and fresh ground pepper to taste. Serve and enjoy.

# Curried Cauliflower & Leeks

serves 4

Roasting cauliflower turns it from plain Jane to delicious diva. With crispy leek ringlets and a little kick of curry spice it's one scrumptious number in my book.


1 large head cauliflower, rinsed, cored, and broken into medium florets

1 large leek, rinsed, white and light green parts cut in 1/2 inch rounds

4 tablespoons extra-virgin olive oil

1 tablespoon good-quality curry powder

1/2 teaspoon sea salt


Preheat oven to 375°. Line baking sheet with parchment paper. Place the cauliflower florets and chopped leek in a large bowl. Drizzle with the olive oil, sprinkle with the curry powder and sea salt, and toss together with hands until the vegetables are evenly coated. Pour onto baking sheet and spread into a single layer. Roast 40–45 minutes, until nicely browned. Serve warm.

# Asparagus Spears with Lemon Zest

serves 4

Asparagus is one of my favorite green vegetables. I like to lightly steam a bunch and have it on hand in the fridge for munching. The taste is so fresh and good that it doesn't lack much in my opinion. The hint of lemon in this dish gives just a touch of zing to entertain the tastebuds.

1 bunch asparagus, trimmed (about 1 pound)

zest of 1 small lemon*

1 tablespoon fresh lemon juice

2 tablespoons olive oil

sea salt and fresh ground pepper

Place asparagus spears in large skillet with just enough water to cover them. Bring to a boil and cook for 2 minutes. Rinse immediately under cold water until asparagus is only slightly warm. Transfer to a large bowl. Add lemon juice, olive oil, salt and pepper to taste. Toss together with hands to thoroughly coat the asparagus. Sprinkle with sea salt and pepper. Place on a serving platter and garnish with fresh lemon zest. Serve and enjoy.

*Chef's Note: I prefer using a zester that makes thin ribbons, but you can also use the traditional kind if you want a finer zest.

# Roasted Brussel Sprouts with Marcona Almonds

serves 4–6

My favorite part of this dish is the way the outer leaves of the brussel sprouts sometimes fall off while roasting and get crispy like little chips – so tasty to munch on!

1 pound brussel sprouts, halved length-wise and ends trimmed

2 tablespoons olive oil

1/2 teaspoon sea salt

1 1/2 tablespoons balsamic vinegar

1/2 cup marcona almonds

Preheat oven to 375°. Line a baking sheet with parchment paper. In a large bowl combine brussel sprouts, olive oil and sea salt, using hands to massage oil and sea salt into the brussel sprouts. Pour onto the baking sheet and spread out in an even layer. Roast for 40–45 minutes, until crisp on the outside and tender on the inside. Transfer to a bowl, add balsamic and toss together with almonds. Sprinkle with sea salt and pepper to taste and serve warm.

# Green Beans & Carrots with Mustard Seeds

serves 4–6

Indian spices offer an exotic twist to the colorful combo of vibrant carrots and green beans. This dish goes great with Indian Spiced Vegetable Curry (page 110).

1 pound green beans, trimmed and cut in half

2 medium carrots, peeled, cut at an angle in 1/4 inch slices

1 small onion, peeled and finely diced

1 tablespoon ghee

1 teaspoon ginger root, peeled and minced

1 teaspoon brown mustard seeds

1 teaspoon turmeric powder

1 teaspoon sea salt

2 tablespoons water

1 1/2 tablespoons lemon juice

Melt ghee in a large skillet over medium heat. Add mustard seeds and turmeric powder and sauté 1–2 minutes until aromatic. Add onions and ginger and sauté until onions are slightly browned. Stir in carrots and sauté for 1 minute. Cover and cook for 5 minutes until slightly tender. Add green beans and sauté for 5 minutes, stirring often. Then add sea salt and water, cover and cook for about 7 minutes or until veggies are tender but still vibrant in color. Add lemon juice and stir. Remove from heat, transfer to a dish and serve.

# Nourished by Plenty

"To know you have enough is to be rich."
- Lao-Tzu, Tao Te Ching

# Grains

Quinoa Tabouli

Crimson Quinoa

Forbidden Black Rice with Roasted Sweet Potato,
Red Pepper & Scallions

Cilantro Rice

Millet & Mushroom Pilaf

Soba Noodles with Black Sesame & Edamame

Butternut Squash & Leek Risotto

Quinoa is my favorite grain. A South American culinary treasure, it was once called "The Gold of the Incas." They recognized its value as a vital energy food. Not only is it higher in protein than many other grains, it's considered a complete protein, meaning it contains all nine essential amino acids. Like many people, when I first made the shift out of the glutenous world of breads and pasta, I was introduced to brown rice, and for awhile we enjoyed a loyal love affair. But then along came quinoa. I was taken by its light, yet hearty consistency and subtle, nutty flavor. Sure, brown rice and I still keep in touch once in awhile, but quinoa has definitely taken its place as my go-to grain.

# Quinoa Tabouli

serves 4–6

Traditional tabouli is made with bulgur, which is a form of wheat. This makes an otherwise fresh and healthy Middle Eastern classic off limits for gluten-free eaters. Luckily, quinoa has a very similar consistency to bulgur and is a great substitute. This is happy news, because tabouli is sensational.

1 cup quinoa, rinsed

1 1/2 cups water

1/4 cup fresh lemon juice

1/4 cup olive oil

1 small cucumber, peeled seeded and finely diced (1 cup)

2 small Roma tomatoes, seeded and finely diced (3/4 cup)

1 cup curly parsley, finely chopped

1/4 cup fresh mint, finely chopped

1/2 cup scallions, thinly sliced

sea salt and fresh ground pepper

Place quinoa, water and a pinch of sea salt in a medium-sized pot. Cover and bring to a boil. Reduce heat and simmer for about 10–15 minutes, until water is absorbed. Meanwhile, prepare cucumber, tomato, herbs and scallions. When quinoa is done transfer to larger glass bowl and set aside to cool. Once cooled, add all remaining ingredients to bowl and thoroughly combine. Taste and add sea and pepper as needed. You can also add more lemon juice if your taste buds crave greater tang.

# Crimson Quinoa

serves 4–6

This dish tends to be a conversation piece because of its flashy appearance. The secret to its colorful flair is... beets!

1 cup quinoa

1 1/2 cups water

1 medium carrot, grated (about 1 cup)

1 small medium red beet, grated (about 1 cup)

1/2 cup flat leaf parsley, chopped

1 1/2 cups fresh spinach or watercress, chopped

1 1/2 tablespoons fresh lemon juice

3 tablespoons olive oil

1/2 teaspoon sea salt


Rinse quinoa and place in medium pot with water and a pinch of sea salt. Bring to a boil, then reduce heat, cover and simmer for 15–20 minutes or until water is absorbed. Meanwhile, wash and grate carrot and beet and put in a large bowl. Wash and chop parsley and greens and add to bowl. When quinoa is done, remove from heat and transfer to bowl with veggies and combine. The heat from the quinoa will slightly blanch the veggies. Add olive oil, lemon juice and sea salt and mix to thoroughly coat all ingredients. Adjust flavor to your liking. This dish can be enjoyed warm, room temperature or chilled.

# Forbidden Black Rice with Roasted Sweet Potato, Red Pepper & Scallions

serves 4–6

Legend has it that this ancient grain was once eaten exclusively by Chinese emperors because it promoted good health and long life. It was so revered that they kept it all to themselves. Luckily, we live in more egalitarian times, and most of us can eat like royalty now. With its unique, nutty flavor and exotic appearance - as well as high levels of iron and antioxidants - black rice is, indeed, a precious gem in the world of grains.

1 cup black rice

1 3/4 cups water

sea salt

2 teaspoons toasted sesame oil

1 medium-large sweet potato, peeled and diced

2 small scallions, white and light green parts sliced thin

1 small red bell pepper, de-seeded and diced small

1 tablespoon tamari

1/2 tablespoon fresh lime juice or brown rice vinegar

Preheat oven to 375°. Rinse rice and transfer to small pot. Add water and a pinch of sea salt. Bring to a boil, then reduce heat and simmer 30 minutes or until liquid is absorbed. While rice is cooking, prep sweet potato, pepper and scallions. Cover baking sheet with parchment paper. Toss sweet potato on baking sheet with 1/2 teaspoon sesame oil and a light sprinkle of sea salt. Place in oven and bake for about 20 minutes or until sweet potatoes are tender and lightly browned. When rice has finished cooking, transfer into a large bowl. In a small bowl, whisk together tamari, lime juice or vinegar, and 1 1/2 teaspoons sesame oil. Pour mixture into bowl with rice. When sweet potatoes are done, add them to rice, along with scallions and red pepper. Stir all ingredients together and taste. Add sea salt and extra lime juice or vinegar to adjust the flavor to your liking.

# Cilantro Rice

serves 4

If you're looking for a tasty rice dish that goes with almost any meal, this is it. Great with Indian, Mexican and Southeast Asian cuisines.


1 cup jasmine rice

1 2/3 cup chicken broth or water

1 teaspoon fresh ginger, peeled and minced

1 1/3 cups fresh cilantro, chopped

1 green onion, thinly sliced

2 tablespoons coconut oil

1 tablespoon toasted sesame oil

1 teaspoon brown rice vinegar


Place rice, liquid and a pinch of sea salt in medium pot and bring to a boil. Cover and reduce heat to low. Simmer rice until tender and all liquid is absorbed, about 15 minutes. Meanwhile, add cilantro, green onion, ginger, oils and vinegar to food processor and blend until almost smooth. Taste and add more sea salt and vinegar as needed. When rice is cooked transfer to a bowl and mix in the cilantro oil, stirring well to thoroughly coat the rice. Serve warm.

# Millet & Mushroom Pilaf

serves 6

Nutrient rich with a sweet, earthy flavor, millet is another wonderful gluten-free grain. Depending on the cooking method, it can be creamy like mashed potatoes or light and fluffy like couscous. In the summer this dish makes a great stuffing for vine-ripe tomatoes. Just carve a hollow inside the tomato – like you would a pumpkin – remove the seeds and juice and stuff with the millet pilaf. Bake at 375° for 10–15 minutes until tomatoes are tender but still hold their shape.

1 cup millet

2 tablespoons ghee

2 cups water or chicken broth

1/4 teaspoon sea salt

1/3 cup minced shallots

8–10 medium crimini mushrooms, washed and thinly sliced

1 small zucchini, washed and grated

1/4 cup chopped chives

1/4 cup chopped fresh herbs, such as dill, basil, cilantro, parsley

1/2 cup crumbled goat cheese (optional)

3 tablespoons olive oil

Heat one tablespoon of the ghee in a medium-sized pot over medium-high heat. Add millet and toast for a few minutes until fragrant. Add water and sea salt and bring to a boil. Reduce heat, cover and simmer for 20–25 minutes. Meanwhile, in a medium-sized skillet, heat the remaining tablespoon of ghee over medium-high heat. Add shallots and sauté for 5 minutes. Then add mushrooms and a sprinkle of sea salt and pepper and sauté until lightly browned, about 6–8 minutes. When millet is done add to mushrooms. Add chives, herbs, zucchini, goat cheese, olive oil and sea salt and pepper to taste. Stir gently together until thoroughly combined. Serve warm or room temperature.

# Soba Noodles with Black Sesame & Edamame

serves 6

Soba is the Japanese name for buckwheat. Although it contains the word "wheat" in its name, buckwheat is totally gluten-free. Check the packaging to make sure you're getting 100% buckwheat. Many companies make their noodles with wheat flour as well. Pure buckwheat noodles are much more delicate, so it's best to cook them gently and serve immediately.

1 box soba noodles - 100% buckwheat

1 cup edamame, shelled and precooked

3 scallions, white and light green parts sliced thin

1/4 cup toasted black sesame seeds

3 tablespoons toasted sesame oil

1/4 cup tamari soy sauce

2 1/2 tablespoons fresh lime juice or brown rice vinegar

Prepare noodles according to instructions on package. While noodles are cooking, wash and prepare scallions. If edamame are frozen, place them in a colander and run under hot water to defrost. Put scallions and edamame in a large bowl. In a small skillet toast the sesame seeds over medium-low heat until they begin to crackle and pop. Stir frequently to help them toast evenly. When noodles are cooked, strain them in a colander and rinse under cold water. Then transfer to the large bowl. In a small bowl whisk together oil, tamari and lime juice or vinegar. Pour mixture over noodles. Add toasted sesame seeds and gently fold all ingredients together using your hands. The edamame sometimes likes to hide out in the bottom of the bowl. They just need a little extra encouragement to come out and play, so you may need to coax them to the surface a bit. Serve immediately at room temperature.

# Butternut Squash & Leek Risotto

serves 4–6

Arborio is an Italian short-grain rice named for the town where it was originally grown. It has a high starch content, which lends to its distinctly creamy consistency and makes every spoonful a luscious treasure.

3 tablespoons ghee

4 cups butternut squash, peeled and cut in 1/2 inch cubes

3 cups leeks, sliced in thin rounds (white and light green parts only)

2 cups arborio rice

7 cups chicken or vegetable broth

3/4 cup freshly grated parmesan cheese (optional)

Melt 2 tablespoons ghee in a large pot over medium-high heat. Add squash and sauté about 5 minutes, until barely tender. Transfer the squash to a bowl and set aside. Reduce heat to medium and add 1 tablespoon of ghee and the leeks. Stir and cook for about 5 minutes, until they're tender but not brown. Add rice and one cup broth. Stirring frequently, simmer until the liquid is absorbed. Add remaining broth in half cup increments, allowing each addition to be absorbed before adding the next. Stir often for about 15–20 minutes. Then add squash and continue to cook about 10 minutes longer. Stir often but gently until rice is just tender and very creamy. Remove from heat and stir in parmesan (optional) and sea salt and freshly ground pepper to taste. Transfer to a large bowl and serve with a sprinkle of grated parmesan on top if you'd like.

Chefs Note: For extra nutrition, in the last five minutes of cooking time, add 3–5 asparagus spears cut into one inch pieces.

# Nourished by Goodness

"The roots of all goodness lie in the soil of
appreciation for goodness."

- Dalai Lama

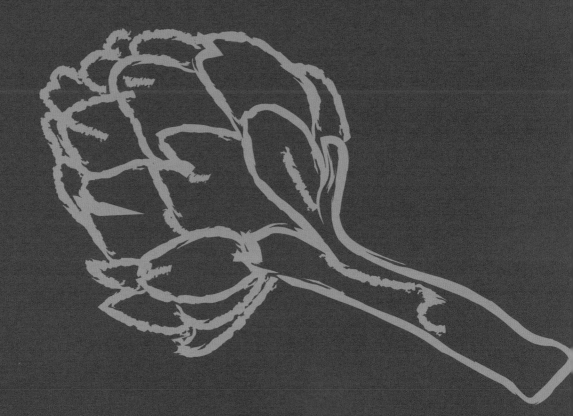

# Vegetarian Main Dishes

Kitchari Patties with Cilantro-Lime Sauce

New World Shepherd's Pie

Polenta Pizza with Artichoke, Olive & Sweet Basil

Butternut Squash Tostadas

Indian Spiced Vegetable Curry

Bhutanese Red Rice & Vegetable Loaf

Stuffed Acorn Squash with Wild Rice and Vegetables

# Kitchari Patties with Cilantro-Lime Sauce

serves 4

Kitchari is a traditional Indian dish made with lentils and rice. Shaped into little patties and lightly pan fried, it transforms into an elegant favorite. Serve with Green Bean & Carrots with Mustard Seeds (page 86) and Roasted Curried Cauliflower (page 80).

1 cup white basmati rice

1/2 cup red lentils

4 cups water

1/2 teaspoon turmeric powder

1 teaspoon sea salt

4 tablespoons ghee

1 tablespoon cumin seeds

1 1/4 cups yellow onion, finely diced

2 teaspoons ginger root, peeled and minced

1/4 cup arrowroot powder

Cilantro-Lime Sauce (see recipe on next page) *make at least 1 hour ahead

Place rice and lentils in a mesh strainer and rinse well. Transfer to a medium-sized pot and add water, turmeric, and sea salt. Cover and bring to a boil. Lower the heat and simmer for about 20–25 minutes or until the water is absorbed.

Meanwhile, melt 2 tablespoons of ghee in a medium-sized skillet over medium-high heat. Add the cumin seeds and sauté for a minute or two until fragrant. Add the onions and ginger and sauté for about 10–12 minutes or until they are slightly browned. Transfer to a large ceramic or glass casserole dish along with the rice and lentil mixture and combine thoroughly. Set aside for about 15–20 minutes and allow to cool, stirring occasionally. On a small plate spread the arrowroot powder. When mixture is cool, form into 8–10 patties (depending on the size you'd like). Lightly dredge the patties in the arrowroot and set aside on a clean surface or plate. Warm 1 tablespoon of ghee in medium-sized skillet over medium-high heat. Add 4–5 patties and fry for about 3–5 minutes each side, until golden brown. Remove from pan and set aside on a clean platter. Add remaining ghee and patties and repeat the process until complete. Serve patties warm with Cilantro-Lime Sauce on top.

**Cilantro-Lime Sauce:**

2 cups cilantro, rinsed and coarsely chopped

1/3 cup  canned coconut milk, (mostly thick cream from top, if possible)

2–3 tablespoons lime juice

1 teaspoon fresh ginger, peeled and minced

1/4 teaspoon sea salt

Combine all ingredients in a blender until creamy smooth. Refrigerate and allow to thicken for at least 1 hour before serving.

# New World Shepherd's Pie

serves 6

Growing up on the east coast, my mother's shepherd's pie was the perfect meal for chilly autumn nights. It was warm and comforting with layers of savory meat, tender vegetables and creamy mashed potatoes. Here I've created a vegetarian version of this childhood favorite using red pepper for a hint of color and mushrooms and walnuts to create a "meaty" texture.

2 cups green beans, trimmed

1 small red bell pepper, sliced in thin strips

1/2 large red onion, peeled and sliced in thin strips

1 cup walnuts, broken into pieces

3 medium portabella mushrooms (6 cups), coarsely chopped

3 garlic cloves, minced

3 tablespoons coconut oil

3 tablespoons tamari

2 teaspoons arrowroot powder

sea salt and fresh ground pepper

Simple Mashed Potatoes (page 79)

Preheat oven to 325°. Place walnut pieces on a baking sheet and roast in the oven for 5–10 minutes being careful not the burn them. You will know they are done when the skin starts to flake. Set walnuts aside.

Next, in a large skillet heat one tablespoon of coconut oil over medium-high heat. Add red onion and sauté for 3–5 minutes. Add peppers to skillet and sauté for 3 minutes. Add green beans, sprinkle with sea salt and pepper and sauté for 5 minutes. Then add 2 tablespoons of water, reduce heat to medium-low, cover and cook for 5 minutes or until green beans are tender crisp. When green beans are done transfer mixture to a bowl, toss with walnuts and set aside. Return skillet to burner, add remaining 2 tablespoons of coconut oil, increase heat to medium-high. Add garlic and sauté 1–2 minutes. Add mushrooms and sauté for 5 minutes. Add 3 tablespoons of tamari and reduce heat to medium. Sauté for 3–5 minutes more, then add arrowroot powder and 2 tablespoons of water. Mix together thoroughly. Transfer mixture to a two-quart baking dish. Spread out evenly to cover bottom of the dish. Add the green bean mixture on top in an even layer. Then finish off with a hearty layer of mashed potatoes. Bake at 365° for 30 minutes. Remove from oven and cool slightly for 5–10 minutes before serving.

# Butternut Squash Tostadas

serves 4

When I make these tostadas the kitchen fills with a wonderful, spicy-sweet aroma. I like to serve them with Avocado Caesar Salad (page 66), whose crisp romaine lettuce and tangy avocado dressing are the perfect complement.

4 cups butternut squash, cut into
1 inch cubes

3 tablespoons coconut oil

1 1/2 tablespoons chili powder

1 1/4 tablespoons cumin powder

2 teaspoons tamari soy sauce

2 cups goat cheddar, grated

2 tablespoons chives or scallions, chopped

1/4 cup pumpkin or sunflower seeds, toasted

4 corn tortillas

Preheat oven to 375°.

Peel the butternut squash, cut in half and use a metal spoon to scoop out seeds and membrane. Cut butternut into 1 inch cubes (4 cups). You will need a large pot and a steamer basket to steam it. Fill the bottom of pot with 2–3 inches of water. Insert steamer basket and add squash. Turn heat to high, cover and steam until tender, about 15 minutes. While squash is steaming grate the cheese and chop the chives or scallions. Toast the seeds in small skillet over medium heat, stirring constantly until golden brown. Once the squash is tender, remove from heat. In a large skillet, heat coconut oil over medium-high heat. Add chili powder and cumin and sauté in oil for 1 minute. Then add the butternut to the skillet. Stir to thoroughly coat the butternut in oil and spices. Sauté the squash for 3 minutes. Add tamari and sauté about 5 minutes more, stirring frequently to help squash break down a bit. The texture will resemble a chunky hash. Remove from heat and set aside. Brush tortillas lightly with a little coconut oil. Place them on a baking sheet and crisp them in the oven for about 5–7 minutes. Remove them from oven and top each tortilla with a layer of the squash mixture. Then sprinkle with cheese and return them to the oven to bake for 10–12 minutes or until cheese is thoroughly melted. Make sure the tortillas don't turn too dark on the bottom. You want them to be lightly browned. The tostadas can then be plated and topped with toasted seeds and chives or scallions. Serve immediately.

# Indian Vegetable Curry with
## Cucumber Raita & Orange Raisin Chutney

serves 6–8

This festive Indian curry adorned with cool, creamy raita and spicy-sweet chutney is a tantalizing feast for the soul and palate. Serve it with warm Cilantro Rice (page 96) for a completely nourishing meal.

**Curry**:

2 tablespoons ghee

2 teaspoons cumin seeds

1 1/4 teaspoons turmeric powder

1 1/4 teaspoons coriander

1 teaspoon fresh ginger, peeled and finely diced

1 small yellow onion, peeled and chopped (1 cup)

3 medium yukon gold potatoes, diced (1 1/2 cups)

1 teaspoon sea salt

1 cup cauliflower, broken into small florets

1 small zucchini, diced (about 1 cup)

1 1/2 cups cooked garbanzo beans (or one 15 ounce can)

1 28 ounce can crushed fire roasted tomatoes

1/2 can coconut milk

In a medium-large pot melt ghee over medium heat. Add cumin seeds, turmeric and coriander and sauté 2 minutes. Add onions and ginger and sauté for 5–7 minutes until onions are translucent and lightly browned. Stir in potatoes and sea salt, cover and cook for 7 minutes, stirring once halfway through. Then stir in cauliflower along with 1/4 cup water. Cover and cook for about 8 minutes until cauliflower and potatoes are slightly tender. Add zucchini and sauté for 5 minutes. Then stir in crushed tomatoes and garbanzo beans. Reduce heat a little, cover and simmer for 10–15 minutes until all vegetables are tender but not mushy. Add coconut milk. Taste and add more sea salt as needed. Serve hot over Cilantro Rice (page 96) with a dollop of Raita and Chutney.

## Cucumber Raita:

1 medium English cucumber, cut in half lengthwise, seeded and grated

2 1/2 cups plain goat or sheep's yogurt

1/4 cup fresh mint, chopped

1/4 cup fresh cilantro, chopped

1/2 teaspoon cumin powder

pinch of sea salt

Mix all ingredients together in a medium bowl and serve. Will keep in the refrigerator for up to a week.

## Orange Raisin Chutney:

1 1/2 cups raisins

2–3 dates pitted

1 orange, peeled and cut into large chunks

1 tablespoon fresh ginger, peeled and minced

1 tablespoon fresh orange peel, coarsely chopped

1/8 teaspoon red chili flakes

pinch of sea salt

Place all ingredients in a food processor using an S-blade and blend until slightly chunky yet smooth.

# Bhutanese Red Rice & Vegetable Loaf

serves 6

This is one of my all time favorite vegetarian dishes. It's hearty and full of savory Asian flavor and goes great with Thai Veggie Salad (page 63).

1 cup Bhutanese red rice

1 1/2 cups water

2 tablespoons tamari

1 tablespoon coconut oil

3 cloves garlic, peeled and minced

2 scallions, thinly sliced

5–6 medium shiitake mushrooms, stems removed and diced small

1/2 red bell pepper, de-seeded and diced small

1 medium carrot, diced small

1 jalapeño, de-seeded, and minced

3 eggs, beaten

1/2 teaspoon toasted sesame oil

3/4 teaspoon sea salt

Preheat oven to 375°. In small pot add rice, water and a pinch of sea salt. Cover and bring to a boil, then reduce heat and simmer for 20 minutes until liquid is absorbed. Meanwhile, prep all vegetables. Beat eggs in small bowl and set aside. In a large skillet, heat coconut oil over medium-high heat. Add garlic and scallions and sauté for 3–4 minutes. Add shiitakes, red pepper, carrot and jalapeño and sauté for 3–5 minutes. Add 1 tablespoon of tamari and sauté 3–5 minutes more, until veggies are slightly tender. Remove skillet from heat and set aside. When rice is done transfer to a large glass or ceramic bowl and allow to cool for 20–30 minutes. After rice has cooled, add beaten eggs and veggies, along with sesame oil and sea salt. Stir well to thoroughly combine. Then pour mixture into a loaf pan and bake for 35–40 minutes. Remove from oven and let stand for 7–10 minutes before slicing and serving.

# Polenta Pizza with Artichoke, Olive & Sweet Basil

serves 4–6

Polenta makes a great edible canvas for tasty pizza masterpieces. The first time I made one I felt like a culinary artist creating a tantalizing feast for the senses. Artichoke and sweet basil is one of my favorite combinations... but it's merely a suggestion. Feel free to unleash your inner Pizza Picasso and devise your own magnum opus.

3 1/2 cups water

1 cup polenta

1/4 teaspoon sea salt

2 tablespoons olive oil

1 cup chunky tomato sauce
 (I like Muir Glen® Organic)

2 cups goat mozzarella cheese, shredded

1 cup marinated artichoke hearts, quartered

10 large fresh basil leaves, torn into
 small pieces

8–10 kalamata olives, pitted and cut in
 half lengthwise

Preheat oven to 400°. In a medium pot bring water to a boil. Add polenta and sea salt and stir well to avoid clumping. Reduce heat to low and simmer for about 20 minutes, stirring occasionally until the liquid is absorbed and polenta is creamy. Transfer polenta to a glass bowl and allow it to cool for 30 minutes. Then transfer polenta to an oiled baking sheet (use olive oil). Using the back of a wooden spoon or rubber spatula, spread the mixture evenly into a 1/2 inch thick rectangle. Spoon 1 tablespoon of olive oil over the polenta and spread across the top with your hands.

Place in oven and bake for about 15 minutes, until bottom begins to turn brown around the edges. Remove from oven and let stand for 5 minutes. Then spread an even layer of tomato sauce over the top. Arrange basil, artichokes and olives in whatever pattern you like and then top with shredded mozzarella. Return to oven and bake an additional 15–20 minutes, until cheese is bubbly and lightly browned.

Let pizza rest for 7–10 minutes then cut into squares and serve.

# Stuffed Acorn Squash with Wild Rice and Vegetables

serves 4

An eye catching, mouthwatering autumn favorite, this dish is a meal all on its own.

2 small acorn squash

1 cup wild rice blend (I like Lundberg Family Farms® brand)

2 cups water

1 tablespoon ghee

1 small yellow onion, peeled & chopped (1 cup)

3 garlic cloves, minced

8 small crimini or button mushrooms, cut in quarters (1 1/2 cups)

1 small carrot, coarsely chopped (1/2 cup)

1 large celery stalk, coarsely chopped (1/2 cup)

1/2 cup crumbled goat cheese (optional)

1/2 teaspoon sea salt

Preheat oven to 375°. Cut squash in half and use a spoon to remove seeds and membrane. Place squash – skin side out – in a large baking dish and add enough water to cover the bottom of the dish, about 1 inch high. Place squash in oven and bake for 30–40 minutes or until they are slightly tender. Meanwhile, rinse the rice and add to a medium-sized pot along with the water. Bring to a boil, then reduce heat, cover and simmer for about 40 minutes or until water is absorbed. While rice and squash are cooking, rinse and chop onions, mushrooms, celery, and carrots. Heat ghee in large skillet over medium-high heat. Add onions and sauté for 3–5 minutes. Add garlic and sauté 3 minutes. Then add mushrooms and sauté for 7 minutes until mushroom start to release their moisture. Add carrots and celery and sauté for 5–7 minutes. When rice is done add to skillet with vegetables. Stir well to combine all ingredients. Remove from heat and set aside to cool slightly. When squash is done, remove from oven and flip them over in the baking dish to ready them for stuffing. If you'd like goat cheese, add it to the rice mixture and fold gently to combine. Then spoon filling into prepared squash, filling generously without over-filling. Once all squash halves are stuffed, return them to the oven and bake for 25–30 minutes more. Remove from oven and let stand for 5 minutes before serving. The first steps of this dish can be done ahead of time and the stuffed squash can refrigerated for up to three days until you are ready to bake it for the final 25–30 minutes and eat. They also freeze well.

# Nourished by Possibility

"In the beginner's mind there are many possibilities,
in the expert's mind there are few."

- Shunryu Suzuki

# Meat, Poultry and Fish

Grilled Marinated Flank Steak

Greek Turkey Meatloaf with Tzatziki Sauce

Lemon-Rosemary Roast Chicken

Moroccan Spiced Chicken Kabobs

Orange-Miso Salmon with Fresh Ginger &
Baby Bok Choy

Halibut Fish Tacos with Mango-Jicama Salsa

The Perfect Salmon with Four Flavors

# Grilled Marinated Flank Steak

serves 4–6

People rave about this steak - it's one of my most requested meat dishes. Giving it enough time in the marinade is well worth it in terms of taste and tenderness. If I have leftovers, I like to top a salad with a few slices of meat to give it a little more substance.


1 (2 pound) flank steak

Marinade:

1/2 cup fresh lime juice

1/2 cup tamari soy sauce

1 tablespoon balsamic vinegar

2 tablespoons olive oil

3 tablespoons toasted sesame oil

2 garlic cloves, minced

sea salt

fresh ground pepper


Place flank steak in 9x11 baking dish. Sprinkle generously with sea salt and pepper. Combine marinade ingredients in a small bowl. Pour marinade over flank steak, cover dish with plastic wrap and refrigerate for at least one hour, but preferably over night. Either way, flip the steak half way through for an even saturation. The longer you marinade the steak the more flavorful it will be. When the flank steak is just about ready, fire up the gas grill to medium-high heat. Cook on the grill for 7–15 minutes each side, depending on your preference. A meat thermometer will read 125° for rare to medium-rare. When meat has reached the desired temperature remove from the grill and place on a cutting board. Let it rest for five minutes before slicing. When slicing cut across the grain using a sharp carving knife.

# Greek Turkey Meatloaf with Tzatziki Sauce

serves 6

This is a satisfying twist on traditional meatloaf that will make your taste buds say "Opa!"

1 tablespoon oil

1 small red onion, diced (1/2 cup)

3 garlic cloves, minced

1 egg, beaten

1 pound ground turkey, dark meat

1/4 cup tomato paste

1 tablespoon fresh oregano leaves

3/4 teaspoon sea salt

1/2 cup almond flour

1/2 cup goat or sheep feta, crumbled

1/4 cup kalamata olives, chopped

1/4 cup sundried tomatoes, chopped

1 cup fresh spinach, chopped

Preheat oven to 350°. Prepare onion, garlic, oregano, olives, sundried tomatoes and spinach. In a small bowl, beat the egg and set aside. In a medium-sized skillet heat oil over medium-high heat. Add diced onion and sauté for 2–3 minutes. Add garlic and sauté 3–5 minutes more. Remove from heat and set aside to cool. In a large bowl combine all ingredients and blend thoroughly with your hands. Transfer into a loaf pan and bake for about 50 minutes or until meat thermometer reads 165°. Serve sliced with tzatziki sauce spooned over the top.

**Tzatziki Sauce:**

1/2 cup plain goat yogurt

1/2 cucumber, finely chopped

1 teaspoon mint, finely chopped

1/8 teaspoon sea salt

2 teaspoons fresh lemon juice

Mix all ingredients together in a bowl, cover and refrigerate until ready to serve. If you have any sauce leftover, you can peel and steam some red beets, lay them on a bed of arugula or spinach, add a sprinkle of sea salt and fresh pepper and top it all off with the tzatziki sauce.

# Lemon-Rosemary Roast Chicken

serves 6

Here in Santa Barbara we have an abundance of citrus and rosemary. Both thrive in the sunshine, and rosemary is a drought tolerant ornamental shrub. This makes for some great urban foraging. Take a late afternoon walk around the block for some fresh air, gather a couple lemons and a few sprigs of rosemary, and voila! You're ready to season your chicken. If you're geographically challenged or at risk of being unneighborly, the farmer's market or grocery store should have what you need.

1 whole chicken, 2–3 pounds

2 whole lemons, 1 cut in half, 1 cut in quarters

2 tablespoons fresh lemon juice

2 tablespoons fresh rosemary, minced

4 sprigs fresh rosemary

2 tablespoons olive oil

2 garlic cloves, minced

coarse sea salt

fresh ground pepper

Preheat oven to 385°. Place chicken in a medium-large baking dish. Stuff the inside of chicken with lemon halves and sprigs of rosemary. Drizzle olive and lemon juice over the chicken. Sprinkle with minced rosemary, fresh ground pepper and a generous amount of coarse sea salt (2–3 tablespoons). Massage seasoning into the skin of the chicken, coating thoroughly. Toss lemon quarters into the baking dish and arrange around the chicken. Bake chicken for 45–60 minutes or until thermometer reads 165°. Remove from oven and allow chicken to stand for 15–30 minutes before slicing. This will help hold in the natural juices and keep the chicken moist.

# Moroccan Spiced Chicken Kabobs

serves 4

Served on a bed of Quinoa Tabouli (page 91) with Lemon Zest Asparagus (page 83), this is one of the most satisfying summertime meals I can think of. If you want to add color, place cherry tomatoes, red onion or bell pepper on the skewers as well. This will also stretch the ingredients to serve more people.

1 1/2 pounds boneless, skinless chicken breast, cut into 3/4 inch cubes

4 long bamboo or metal skewers

Marinade:

1 teaspoon paprika

1 teaspoon chili powder

1 teaspoon cumin powder

1/2 teaspoon sea salt

2 tablespoons olive oil

2 tablespoons lemon juice

2 cloves garlic, peeled and minced

Place cubed chicken in large casserole dish and set aside. To make marinade, combine spices, olive oil, lemon juice and garlic together in a small bowl. Pour mixture over chicken and, using your hands, thoroughly coat chicken with marinade. Refrigerate for at least 1 hour. Skewer the marinated chicken and grill 5–7 minutes each side until cooked through.

# Orange-Miso Salmon with Fresh Ginger & Baby Bok Choy

serves 2

I don't know what I love best about this dish. The divine, succulent texture of the salmon or the intoxicating flavor fusion of orange, ginger and toasted sesame. It's all so good.

4 baby bok choy bunches, cut length-wise and quartered

1/2 cup cilantro, stems removed

2 scallions, white and light green parts thinly sliced

2 tablespoons orange peel, cut in thin strips

2 teaspoons fresh ginger, peeled and cut in thin strips

1 pound wild Alaskan salmon, cut in two pieces

**Marinade:**

1/4 cup red miso paste

2 tablespoons fresh orange juice

2 tablespoons fresh lime juice

1 1/2 tablespoons tamari

2 teaspoons toasted sesame oil

sea salt

parchment paper

Preheat oven to 400°. In a small bowl, whisk together marinade ingredients and set aside. Cut two 13 x 9 pieces of parchment paper. Place bok choy and half the ginger, orange peel, cilantro and scallions on the bottom of each piece of parchment. Save the other half of the ingredients for the top of the salmon. Next, lay the salmon on top of bok choy. Sprinkle lightly with sea salt. Pour marinade over each piece of fish. Then top with remaining ginger and orange peel. Fold parchment paper over the fish and crimp the edges together for a tight seal. Place the parchment pockets on a baking sheet and bake salmon for 12 minutes. Then place parchment pockets on plates and unwrap to expose the salmon. Sprinkle with remaining scallions and cilantro. Serve hot with Forbidden Black Rice (page 94) or Sesame Soba Noodles (page 98).

# Halibut Fish Tacos with Mango-Jicama Salsa

serves 4–6

This dish is full of zesty, festive flavors and is easy to whip together for a casual dinner party with friends.

3 tablespoons coconut oil

1 small red onion, halved and cut in thin strips

3 cloves of garlic, peeled and minced

1 medium jalapeño, membrane and seeds removed, finely diced

1 small red bell pepper, membrane and seeds removed, cut into thin strips

1 small yellow bell pepper, membrane and seeds removed, cut into thin strips

1 1/4 pounds wild Alaskan halibut

1 1/4 teaspoons chili powder

1 teaspoon cumin powder

sea salt and fresh ground pepper

1 tablespoon fresh lime juice

1 cup fresh cilantro, coarsely chopped

1 dozen corn tortillas

coconut oil for warming tortillas

Melt 1 tablespoon coconut oil in large skillet over medium-high heat. Add onions and sauté for about 7 minutes until they begin to brown. Add garlic, jalapeño and bell pepper and sauté for about 10 minutes, until peppers and onions are nicely browned and tender. Transfer to a bowl and set aside. Add remaining 2 tablespoon coconut oil to skillet. Add spices and sauté for 1–2 minutes. Then place fish in skillet, reduce heat slightly if too hot. Cook fish for 5 minutes then flip and cook other side for another 5 minutes. With a spatula or wooden spoon begin to break fish into hunks while cooking. Sprinkle with sea salt and pepper and sauté until fish is just barely translucent. Then return pepper/onion mixture plus cilantro and lime juice to skillet and gently fold all ingredients together while cooking for an additional 3–5 minutes. Be careful not to over-cook the fish. Remove from heat, cover and set aside. Warm tortillas in a clean skillet with small amount of coconut oil, 2–3 minutes each side. Fill tortillas with halibut mixture and serve with a side of fresh Mango-Jicama Salsa (see recipe on next page).

**Mango-Jicama Salsa:**

1 ripe mango, pitted, peeled and diced

1 avocado pitted, peeled and diced

1 tomato, diced

1/4 cup jicama, peeled and diced

1 jalapeño, seeded and minced

1/2 cup red onion, peeled and minced

1/4 cup chopped cilantro

1 lime, juiced

1 tablespoon olive oil

1/4 teaspoon cumin powder

sea salt

Mix all ingredients together in a medium bowl and enjoy!

# The Perfect Salmon with Four Flavors

serves 4

This foolproof way of preparing salmon guarantees that it will always turn out slightly crisp on the outside and moist and tender on the inside - otherwise known as perfect.


4 (6 ounce) wild salmon fillets

olive oil

sea salt & fresh ground pepper


To prepare the salmon:

Preheat oven to 450°. Heat 2-3 tablespoons olive oil in oven-proof skillet over high heat for 4 minutes. Meanwhile, rub both sides of the salmon fillets with olive oil and season the tops generously with sea salt and fresh ground pepper. When the pan is very hot, place the salmon fillets flesh side down in the pan and cook over medium heat without moving them for 2 minutes, until they're very browned. Carefully turn the fillets over and place the pan in the oven for 7–10 minutes more, until the salmon is barely cooked through. Serve with one of the four flavors.

**Flavor One: Dill-Pistachio Pesto**

1/3 cup fresh dill, finely chopped

2 small green onions, trimmed and chopped

1 small clove garlic, peeled and minced (1/2 teaspoon)

1/2 cup pistachios, toasted and finely chopped

1/4 cup olive oil

1/2 teaspoon lemon juice

generous pinch of sea salt

Combine all ingredients together in a small bowl. Mix well to thoroughly combine. Spoon over top of prepared salmon fillets

**Flavor Two: Fava Bean Succotash**

1 1/2 pounds fava beans, shelled (you can substitute 1 1/2 cups frozen lima beans, thawed)

2 large ears of corn, kernels cut off the cob (about 2 cups)

1 large tomato, seeded, diced

2–3 tablespoons chopped fresh Italian parsley

1 small clove garlic, peeled and minced

1 teaspoon lemon juice

1 tablespoon extra-virgin olive oil

Cook fava beans in a medium-large pot of salted, boiling water until just tender, about 5 minutes. Using a slotted spoon, transfer beans to a colander; reserve cooking water. Rinse beans with cold water. Then peel off outer skins of beans and discard, placing beans in a medium bowl. Add corn kernels to reserved cooking water and cook about 1–2 minutes, then drain in a colander. Return beans and corn to the pot. Mix in tomato, Italian parsley, garlic, lemon juice and olive oil. Season to taste with salt and pepper. Spoon onto a serving platter or individual plates and lay the prepared salmon on top. Sprinkled extra parsley on top as a garnish.

## vor Three: Roasted Red Pepper & Artichoke Tapenade

ı (7 ounce) jar roasted red peppers, drained and chopped

1 (6 ounce) jar marinated artichoke hearts, drained and chopped

1/2 cup fresh cilantro, finely chopped

1 tablespoon Italian parsley, finely chopped

1/2 cup freshly grated Pecorino Romano cheese

1/3 cup olive oil

1/4 cup capers, drained

3 cloves garlic, peeled and minced

1 tablespoon fresh lemon juice

 sea salt and fresh ground pepper


Blend all ingredients together in a food processor. Transfer to a bowl and add sea salt and pepper to taste. Refrigerate at least two hours to allow flavors to blend. Spoon over prepared salmon fillets and serve.


## Flavor Four: Asian Apricot Glaze

5 tablespoons apricot preserves (I like Sorrel Ridge® 100% Fruit Spread, no sugar)

1/4 cup red miso paste

1/4 cup brown rice or white wine vinegar

1 1/2 teaspoons orange peel, finely grated

1/2 teaspoon ginger, peeled and minced

1 small clove garlic, peeled and minced


Combine all ingredients in a small pot and heat on medium until sauce thickens, about 3 minutes. Spoon over top of prepared salmon fillets and serve.

# Nourished by Delight

"Joy is what happens to us when we allow ourselves
to recognize how good things really are."
                              - Marianne Williamson

# Sweet Treats and Desserts

Peach-Blackberry Crumble

Chocolate Velvet Pie with Pecan Coconut Crust

Coconut Tapioca Pudding

Ginger Molasses Cake with Coconut Cashew Cream

Mexican Chocolate Cherry Cookies

Lavender Hazelnut Shortbread

Banana Maple Oaties

Almond-Goji Berry Energy Balls

# Peach–Blackberry Crumble

serves 6

This crumble is a real crowd pleaser. It's great for potlucks and casual dinner parties. To keep it seasonal you can substitute other fruits such as apple, pear and strawberries.

**Fruit Mixture:**

6 large peaches cut into thin slices

1 1/2 cups blackberries

2 tablespoons maple syrup

1/2 teaspoon cinnamon

1 teaspoon ginger powder

**Topping:**

2 1/2 cups gluten-free oats

1/2 cup + 1 tablespoon gluten-free oat flour

1 cup pecans - coarsely chopped

3/4 teaspoon sea salt

1/2 teaspoon ginger powder

1 teaspoon cinnamon

1/2 cup maple syrup

1/2 cup coconut oil, melted

Preheat oven to 350°. Put sliced peaches in a medium-sized bowl. Add blackberries, maple syrup, cinnamon and ginger. Gently stir together. Transfer fruit mixture to a baking dish and set aside.

For the crumble topping, mix all ingredients together in a medium-sized bowl until well blended. Pour topping over fruit mixture and spread evenly to cover the fruit.

Bake for 40 minutes or until crumble turns golden brown.

# Chocolate Velvet Pie with Pecan Coconut Crust

serves 8–10

If you're in the mood for something utterly ecstatic, here it is. One of my friends who isn't particularly a "sweets" person took a bite of this pie and broke into hoots and hops of uncontrollable delight. Serve it in small slices – a little goes a long way.

**Crust:**

2 cups pecans

1/3 cup shredded coconut

8 to 10 medjool dates, pitted

1 1/2 tablespoons virgin coconut oil

1/4 teaspoon cardamom powder

1 tablespoon cinnamon

**Toppings:**

3/4 cup raw cacao nibs

1/2 cup shredded coconut

fresh berries

**Filling:**

1 cup raw cashew butter

1 small avocado

½ cup + 2 tablespoon cocoa powder

½ cup maple syrup

½ cup slightly melted coconut butter – not too melted or mixture will be liquidy

¼ cup water

1 tablespoon vanilla extract

Place nuts into a food processor and pulse until finely ground. Then add remaining crust ingredients and pulse until thoroughly ground and mixed. Press crust mixture into the bottom of a 9.5 inch deep-dish pie plate. Put in refrigerator to chill for at least an hour. Add 1/2 cup cocoa powder and all other filling ingredients into food processor and blend until creamy smooth. Taste and if you'd like a stronger chocolate flavor add 1 tablespoon of cocoa powder at a time to your liking. Pour chocolate filling into the pie plate. Spread evenly with a rubber spatula and decorate with your toppings. Place your creation in the refrigerator to chill for 3–4 hours. Slice and serve.

# Coconut Tapioca Pudding

serves 8

I was fascinated to discover that the root of the cassava plant, which tapioca is derived from, contains cyanide. The ancient Mayans figured out a way to extract the poison for their blow darts, leaving the roots uncontaminated and edible. I can almost see Mother Nature winking as she reminds us that life is a beautiful and bizarre paradox... and that everything is of use.

1 cup small tapioca pearls

3 1/2 cups water

large pinch of sea salt

1 can coconut milk

1/2 cup maple syrup

2–3 ripe mangos, peeled and diced

Cover the tapioca with lukewarm water for 15–20 minutes or until the granules expand and soften. Drain in a mesh strainer. Place tapioca, pinch of salt and 3 1/2 cups water in a pot over high heat. Bring to a boil. Reduce heat to medium-low and simmer 10–15 minutes. Stir occasionally, adding a little more water (if necessary) to prevent tapioca from bubbling and "spitting." When tapioca turns soft and a little gooey, switch off heat and cover. Let tapioca sit 10 minutes - the residual heat inside the tapioca will finish cooking the pearls until they're soft and translucent. Stir in coconut milk and maple syrup. Transfer tapioca to a glass storage container. Allow to cool, then cover with a lid and let chill in the refrigerator for at least an hour. Spoon tapioca into small bowls and crown each serving with fresh mango.

# Ginger Molasses Cake with Coconut Cashew Cream

serves 12

One bite of this satisfying cake is guaranteed to evoke fond memories of Christmas cheer. And while it's a true holiday pleaser, its sweet, spicy flare is well received any time of the year.

2 cups of gluten-free oat flour, sifted

1/2 teaspoon baking soda

1/2 teaspoon sea salt

1 1/2 tablespoons ground ginger

1/4 teaspoon ground cinnamon

1/2 teaspoon ground cloves

1/2 cup molasses

1 cup maple syrup

1/2 cup coconut oil, melted

2/3 cup canned coconut milk

2 eggs, beaten

1 tablespoon apple cider vinegar

1 tablespoon vanilla extract

Preheat oven to 350°. Lightly grease an 8 x 8 baking pan with coconut oil.

In a medium-sized bowl add all dry ingredients, blend well and set aside. In a blender add all wet ingredients and blend on low speed until well combined. Pour wet mix into dry mix and stir or whisk until you have a smooth batter.

Pour batter into greased baking pan and place in the preheated oven. Bake for about 45–50 minutes or until cake is firm yet springy in the middle and the edges pull slightly away from the pan. Let cool for about 15 minutes. Then cut into squares, top with a dollop of Coconut Cashew Cream (recipe below) and serve.

**Coconut Cashew Cream:**

makes about 2 cups

2 cups raw cashews, soaked in water for 6–8 hours

1 cup canned coconut milk

5 dates, pitted

generous pinch of cardamom powder

Pour canned coconut milk into the blender first; this will help ingredients blend with ease. Drain and rinse soaked cashews and add them to blender along with the dates and cardamom. Blend thoroughly on high until mixture is creamy smooth. Transfer into a small bowl. You can make this ahead of time and store in the refrigerator for up to three days.

# Mexican Chocolate Cherry Cookies

makes 2 dozen

I have one word for these cookies: Scrumdiddleyumptuous!

2 3/4 cups blanched almond flour

1/2 teaspoon sea salt

1/2 teaspoon baking soda

1/4 cup unsweetened cocoa powder

1/2 teaspoon cinnamon

generous pinch of cayenne (optional)

1/2 cup coconut oil (melted)

3/4 cup maple syrup

1 tablespoon vanilla extract

1 cup dark chocolate chips

1 cup dried cherries

Preheat oven to 350°. Line two large baking sheets with parchment paper.

In a large bowl combine the almond flour, sea salt, baking soda, cocoa powder and spices. In a medium bowl whisk together coconut oil, maple syrup, and vanilla. Then fold the wet ingredients into the almond flour mixture until thoroughly blended. Add chocolate chips and cherries and fold into batter. Spoon in heaping tablespoon-sized amounts onto prepared baking sheets, spacing about 2 inches apart. Bake for 10–15 minutes, until tops of cookies look slightly crisp - be careful not to over-bake! Let the cookies rest on baking sheet for 10–15 minutes, then remove with a spatula and serve warm with a glass of fresh coconut or almond milk.

# Lavender Hazelnut Shortbread Cookies

makes 2 dozen

Light and luxurious with hints of hazelnuts and lavender essence, these cookies are the perfect complement to a warm pot of afternoon tea.

2 1/2 cups blanched almond flour

1/2 teaspoon sea salt

1/2 teaspoon baking soda

1 cup hazelnuts, toasted and coarsely chopped

1 tablespoon culinary lavender

1/2 cup coconut oil, melted

5 tablespoons maple syrup

1 tablespoon vanilla extract

Preheat oven to 350°. Line two baking sheets with parchment paper. Place hazelnuts on a baking sheet and bake them for 10–15 minutes, until they are fragrant and lightly browned. Place the toasted nuts on a clean dishtowel. Fold the dishtowel over (or use another one on the top) and rub the nuts vigorously. The skins will loosen and fall off. When nuts have cooled, coarsely chop and place them in a large bowl along with the almond flour, sea salt, baking soda, and lavender. In a medium bowl whisk together coconut oil, maple syrup and vanilla. Add the wet ingredients to the almond flour mixture and blend with a wooden spoon until thoroughly combined. Roll the dough into a log 2 1/2 inches in diameter. Wrap it in parchment paper and place in the freezer for one hour or until firm. Then remove the log from freezer, unwrap and slice into 1/4 inch thick rounds. Place the rounds on baking sheets, leaving 2 inch space between each cookie. Bake for 8–10 minutes or until lightly brown around the edges. Let cookies cool for 20 minutes and then remove with a spatula and serve with a warm pot of your favorite tea.

# Banana Maple Oaties

makes 2 dozen

These little cookies are quite cute and good natured. Perfect for cookie monsters and hungry hobbits looking for a wholesome treat.

1 cup softened virgin coconut oil

1 large ripe banana, mashed (1 cup)

1 1/2 cups maple sugar

1/4 cup ground flax seeds

1 tablespoon vanilla extract

3 cups gluten-free oat flour

1 cup gluten-free rolled oats

3/4 teaspoon baking soda

3/4 teaspoon sea salt

1 teaspoon cinnamon

Preheat oven to 350°. In a large bowl mash the banana with a fork. Add coconut oil, maple sugar, ground flax seeds and vanilla extract and stir well to combine. In a medium bowl combine remaining ingredients. Add dry mixture to the large bowl and fold together with rubber spatula until thoroughly mixed. Drop batter in heaping spoonfuls onto an ungreased cookie sheet, leaving about an inch and a half in between. Bake for 12 to 15 minutes or until slightly golden around the edges. Remove cookies and allow them to cool for about 10 minutes before serving.

# Almond-Goji Berry Energy Balls

makes about 30

A satisfying and nutritious treat for all ages. These are the perfect grab-and-go healthy snack. They may be small and cute... but watch out! They pack a mighty taste and energy punch.

2 cups chunky roasted almond butter

2–3 tablespoons coconut oil, melted

1/2 cup maple syrup

1 cup rolled oats

1 cup dried and shredded coconut + more for coating

3/4 cups dried goji berries

1/2 cup raisins

1/4 cup pecans, chopped

2 tablespoons sesame seeds

1 tablespoon maca powder

3/4 teaspoon cinnamon

3/4 teaspoon ground ginger

1/4 teaspoon sea salt

In a medium-large bowl combine all ingredients. Use hands to mix thoroughly and form into a large ball. Form the mixture into small balls. Put about 1 cup of shredded coconut on small plate. Roll balls in the coconut and place them in an airtight container. Store in the refrigerator for up to 10 days.

# Nourished by Kindness

"May the long time sun shine upon you, all love surround you, and the pure light within you guide your way on."

- Irish Blessing

# Extra Surprises

Almond Bread

Rosemary Three Seed Crackers

Kale Crisps

Carrot Butter

Kalamata Olive Hummus

Ghee

Gomasio

# Almond Bread

makes 1 loaf

This bread is best when warm and smeared with Carrot Butter (page 152) or ghee. It's fun to experiment with different additions, such as cinnamon and raisins or rosemary and roasted garlic. Use your imagination and see what delicious flavors you can come up with.

1 pound raw almonds (3 1/4 cups)

2 eggs, beaten

1 1/2 teaspoons baking soda

1/2 teaspoon sea salt

1 tablespoon olive oil

3/4 cup sparkling water

In a food processor, grind almonds to a fine meal. In a large bowl, combine almond meal with the remaining ingredients: eggs, baking soda, salt, olive oil, and sparkling water. Fold together until well combined. Add the mixture to a lightly greased loaf pan and bake at 350° for 1 hour. Let cool for 10 minutes. Slice and enjoy!

# Rosemary Three Seed Crackers

## makes about three-dozen

Most crackers are made with wheat or some form of gluten, which makes snacking a bit challenging when you have gluten or wheat sensitivity. Luckily these tasty little crackers are the perfect solution.

2 cups blanched almond flour

2 teaspoons sea salt

1 cup ground flax meal

1 cup sesame seeds

1 cup pumpkin seeds

1 teaspoon garlic granules

1 1/2 tablespoons fresh rosemary, finely chopped

3 tablespoons coconut oil, melted

3 large eggs, beaten

Preheat the oven to 350°. Set aside three baking sheets. Cut pieces of parchment paper to fit the three baking sheets. In a large bowl, combine all dry ingredients. In a medium bowl, whisk together beaten eggs and coconut oil. Stir the wet ingredients into the dry ingredients. Use hands to thoroughly combine.

Divide dough into three balls and place on baking sheets. Press each ball down to about 1/8 inch flatness. Using a pizza cutter or sharp knife, cut dough into 2 inch squares. Slightly separate each square so they don't get stuck together.

Bake for about 15 minutes, until lightly golden brown. Let the crackers cool for 20–30 minutes before removing from baking sheets. Store in an airtight container to keep them fresh and crisp.

# Kale Crisps

These make a tasty chip-like snack that even kids enjoy. Once baked they become light and crispy, making them fun munchies. The lemon and garlic add some tang and zip.

1 bunch curly kale

1/2 teaspoon sea salt

2 tablespoons oil (olive or coconut)

1/4 teaspoon garlic powder

2 teaspoons fresh lemon juice

Preheat oven to 325°. In a large bowl combine all ingredients with hands. Cover a baking sheet with parchment paper and spread kale out evenly over the baking sheet. Bake for 12 minutes. Flip it with a spatula and bake 6–8 minutes more, until the kale turns crisp and lightly brown.

# Carrot Butter

makes about 2 1/4 cups

You can whip this up in a snap as a wonderful spread for Almond Bread (page 148), Rosemary Three Seed Crackers (page 149) or as a dip for raw veggies.

2 cups carrots, diced

1/4 cup tahini

1/2 cup carrot water

1/2 teaspoon sea salt

Place carrots and water in a medium-sized pot and bring to a boil. Reduce heat and simmer until the carrots are tender, about 5 minutes. Strain carrots, reserving 1/2 cup of the boiled water. Add tahini, carrots, reserved water and salt to a blender and blend until creamy smooth. Transfer to a glass jar. Will firm upon chilling and will keep for up to a week in the refrigerator.

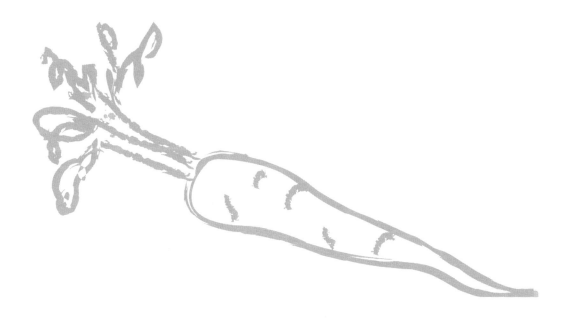

# Kalamata Olive Hummus

serves 4–6

Hummus is a great protein snack to have on hand, and raw vegetables or Rosemary Three Seed Crackers (page 149) make a great vehicle for it. When I need to fuel up but I'm not quite hungry enough for a full meal it's the perfect thing. Try it without the olives for a kid-friendly snack.

2 cups cooked garbanzo beans (if you're short on time use a 15 ounce can of
   garbanzo beans instead)

1 medium clove of garlic, peeled

1/4 cup water

1/4 cup olive oil

1/4 cup fresh lemon juice

2 tablespoons tahini

1 1/2 teaspoons sea salt + 1/2 teaspoon for salting garbanzo bean cooking water

12 kalamata olives, pitted

pinch of paprika

Soak garbanzo beans overnight, drain and rinse. Place them in a small pot, cover with salted water, about 2–3 inches above beans. Bring to a boil, then reduce heat to low and simmer. Stir occasionally until garbanzos are thoroughly cooked but not mushy, about one hour. Drain and allow to cool. Place garlic in food processor with S-blade and pulse until coarsely chopped. Add garbanzo beans (set aside 6–10 beans for garnish), olive oil, water, lemon juice, tahini, sea salt and 4–5 olives to food processor. Blend ingredients until creamy smooth. Transfer to a bowl. Coarsely chop the remaining olives and fold into hummus mixture. Taste and adjust flavor to your liking with lemon or sea salt. Top with remaining garbanzo beans, a drizzle of olive oil and a pinch of paprika. Serve with sliced cucumber.

# Ghee

makes 1 1/2 cups

Ghee is unsalted butter without the hard-to-digest, cholesterol-forming milk solids. It's a staple in traditional Ayruvedic cooking and is great for high temperature cooking. Not to mention, its uniquely delicious flavor is oh-so-good when spread on Almond Bread (page 148) or melted and drizzled over popcorn.

1 pound unsalted butter

Place butter in small saucepan and gently heat over medium-low. When butter separates into two layers and foam appears on the surface, skim foamy layer off with a spoon. Then place a piece of cheesecloth over the mouth of a jar and carefully pour the clear golden liquid into the jar. The milk solids should remain at the bottom of the pan. Cover tightly with lid. Ghee will keep 1–2 months at room temperature and 2–3 months in the refrigerator.

# Gomasio

This Japanese condiment is used in macrobiotic cooking as a more healthful alternative to table salt. I like to sprinkle it on steamed veggies, scrambled eggs and other savory dishes.

2 cups raw, unhulled sesame seeds

1 tablespoon sea salt

Place sesame seeds in a large cast iron skillet over medium heat. Roast for about 10 minutes, stirring constantly until seeds are golden brown. Transfer into a bowl and stir in sea salt. Then place in food processor and pulse lightly to create a coarse meal. When completely cool transfer gomasio to a glass jar. It will keep for up to 6 weeks.

# Sources

Here is a wonderful array of premium purveyors to consider as you stock your all-natural pantry.

## Arrowhead Mills

www.arrowheadmills.com

Organic baking mixes, grains, cereals, and nut butters, many of which are gluten-free.

## Artisana

www.artisana.com

Raw, organic nut and seed butters and spreads - including my favorite coconut butter.

## Bob's Red Mill

www.bobsredmill.com

Alternative, gluten-free flours and baking mixes - mostly organic.

## Coombs Family Farms

www.coombsfamilyfarms.com

Pure, organic maple syrup and maple sugar.

## Dagoba

www.dagoba.com

Organic fair trade chocolate products, including organic cocoa powder.

## Eden Organics

www.edenfoods.com

A variety of macrobiotic foods such as seaweeds, miso paste, sea salts, soba noodles and more.

## Essential Living Foods

www.essentiallivingfoods.com

They make a great gluten-free flour blend and other fabulous organic products.

## Flavorganics

www.flavorganics.com

High-quality, organic extracts.

## Glenmuir

www.glenmuir.com

Organic, field-grown, vine ripened tomatoes, sauces and more.

## Lotus Foods

www.lotusfoods.com

Exotic, organic heirloom rice from around the world.

## Napa Valley Naturals

www.napavalleynaturals.com

Fine organic olive oils and vinegars.

## Nutiva

www.nutiva.com

The best organic coconut oil, hemp oil and hemp protein.

## Rapunzel

www.rapunzel.com

They make great vegetable bouillon cubes, with or without sea salt. Perfect for a quick soup starter.

## Redwood Hill Farms

www.redwoodhillfarms.com

Fine goat milk products, such as yogurt and various cheeses.

## San- J

www.san-j.com

Organic, gluten-free tamari soy sauce.

## Spectrum

www.spectrumorganics.com

Select organic and artisanal cooking oils and vinegars from around the world.

## Spicely Organic Spices

www.spicely.com

All natural, 100% organic culinary herbs and spices.

## Sunridge Farms

www.sunridgefarms.com

Organic dried fruits, nuts and seeds.

## Tinkyada

www.tinkyada.com

A variety of organic, gluten-free rice pasta with amazing texture and taste.

## Wholesome Sweetners

www.wholesomesweeteners.com

Organic sugars, blackstrap molasses and agave nectar.

## Recommended Reading and Resources:

*Animal, Vegetable, Miracle* - Barbara Kingsolver
*Comfortable with Uncertainty* - Pema Chödrön
*Full Moon Feast* - Jessica Prentice
*Healing with Whole Foods* - Paul Pitchford
*In Buddha's Kitchen* - Kimberley Snow
*In Defense of Food* - Michael Pollan
*The New Whole Foods Encyclopedia* - Rebecca Wood

www.localharvest.org
www.organicconsumers.org
www.seedsofchange.com
www.slowfood.com

# Index

163

# A Gift of Love

A portion of the proceeds from every cookbook sold will be donated to select organizations devoted to providing hunger relief and sustainable living skills to those in need around the world and right here in our own backyard. To learn more about the organizations and projects you are helping to support visit www.nourishedbylife.com and see who we are donating to this month!

12940018R00092

Made in the USA
Charleston, SC
07 June 2012